The Beginner's Bible to Fly Fishing

Fly Fishing Guide

Bill Perry
Daniel Bryant
Greg Tanaka

Contents

1 Why Fly Fishing 1
2 The Fly Rod 4
3 The Fly Reel 10
4 The Fly Line 15
5 Knots 19
6 Terminal Tackle 26
7 Fly Rod Rigging 38
8 Fly Casting 45
9 Presentation and Specialty Casts 52
10 Fly Fishing Apparel & Accessories 59
11 Reading a Trout Stream 80
12 Dry Fly Fishing 86
13 Nymph Fishing 88
14 Streamer Fishing 91
15 Hooking – Playing – Landing Trout 93
16 A Trout's Diet 101
17 Trout Identification 123
18 Conclusion 127
19 About the Authors & Map the Xperience 128
Fly Fishing Terminology 131

Copyright © 2025

Daniel Bryant and Bill Perry

All rights reserved. No part of this publication may be reproduced, distributed, or transmitted in any form or by any means, including photocopying, recording, or other electronic or mechanical methods without the prior written permission of the publisher. For permission requests, contact the publisher via the address below.

Map the Xperience, LLC
PO Box 7085 Avon, CO 81620
www.mapthexperience.com

Preface

Fly fishing is more than just a pastime—it's a journey into nature, patience, and skill. Whether you are standing knee-deep in a mountain stream or casting into a calm lake at dawn, fly fishing offers a unique connection to the world around us. The rhythm of the cast, the whisper of the line, and the anticipation of a strike create a meditative experience that captivates beginners and seasoned anglers alike.

This book, *The Beginner's Bible to Fly Fishing*, is designed to introduce you to the fundamentals of fly fishing. From understanding essential gear to mastering casting techniques, you will find practical guidance to help you get started. Beyond the mechanics, you'll discover the art and philosophy of fly fishing—a pursuit that teaches patience, respect for nature, respect for other fishermen, and a sense of adventure.

As you embark on this journey, remember that fly fishing is as much about the experience as it is about the catch. The stories shared on the water, the lessons learned in quiet moments, and the beauty of nature will leave a lasting impression. So, gear up, step into the water, and let the river teach you its timeless lessons.

This is the first book in a series. Following books will expand on certain fly fishing techniques and strategies

Tight lines and happy fly fishing, Bill Perry and Daniel Bryant

1
Why Fly Fishing

The river is alive. It moves, breathes, and speaks in whispers only the keenest ears can hear. To some, it's just water flowing over rocks. To others, like Bill Perry, it's a classroom, a sanctuary, and an old friend. Bill has spent a lifetime listening to the river's stories, learning its secrets, and teaching others how to do the same. If you're here, reading this, then perhaps you, too, have heard its call. Welcome.

We're Bill Perry and Daniel Bryant, and if you've ever wanted to learn fly fishing without feeling like you need a PhD in knots, entomology, and river physics—then you've found the right book. Fly fishing is one of the most rewarding and downright addictive ways to catch fish, and trust us, it's nowhere near as complicated as some folks make it sound.

Sure, there's a bit of a learning curve (we won't lie), but that's why we're here. Think of Bill as your wise master—an angler who has spent decades mastering the art of fly fishing and teaching others to do the same. Bill is a former owner and operator of Fly Fishing Outfitters for almost twenty years, a two-time Orvis Outfitter of the Year, and a Colorado Master Angler. He holds an IFGA World Record. He has guided thousands of anglers, taught fly fishing at Colorado Mountain College for two decades, and even served as a founding board member of the Eagle River Coalition. He has administered over 10,000 trips, some as large as 400 fly fishers. With over 20,000 commercial river miles under his belt and extensive experience running guide training schools and rowing certification programs, Bill has seen it all. Some people pick up fly fishing in minutes, others take a little longer (there's no shame in getting tangled now and then). But there's one universal truth: once people give fly fishing a real shot, they almost always fall in love with it. We're going to take you through this book just like a college course—except there are no exams, no stress, and best of all, everyone gets an A. Think of it as Fly Fishing 101, where we break things down step by step, making the learning process smooth, enjoyable, and rewarding. Whether you're a total beginner or have some experience on the water, by the time you finish, you'll have the knowledge and confidence to cast, present, and fish like a pro.

So, What's the Big Deal About Fly Fishing?

Unlike traditional fishing—where the weight of your lure carries your line out—fly fishing flips the script. Here, the line is weighted, and the fly (a tiny, almost weightless imitation of an insect) simply goes along for the ride. Sounds fancy, right? It is, but it's also pure artistry. Once you get the hang of it, casting a fly rod feels more like a dance than a science. There's rhythm, precision, and just the right amount of flick-of-the-wrist magic involved.

Fly fishing is more than just casting, though. It's about understanding the river, the fish, the insects, and the delicate balance between man and nature. It's about patience and presence. Every time you step into the water, you're stepping into something much bigger than yourself. Fly fishing is a sport you can grow into and never grow out of. Whether you're just getting started or have been casting for years, there's always something new to learn, another challenge to take on, and a deeper connection to the water waiting to be discovered. It's a lifelong journey—one that keeps you coming back, season after season.

More Than Just Fishing

Here's the thing: fly fishing isn't just about catching fish (though that's certainly a nice bonus). For some, it's a sport—a challenge to master. For others, it's a form of meditation, a way to escape the noise of the world and just be in the moment.

Fly fishing is more than just technique or matching the hatch—it's an experience that engages all the senses. The steady flow of the river, the play of light on the water, the feel of the rod in your hands, and the crisp scent of the outdoors all come together to make it something deeper than just fishing. It's this connection to the water and the world around you that makes fly fishing truly special.

Your Journey Starts Here

Our goal with this book is simple: to make fly fishing approachable, understandable, and most of all—fun. We'll break down everything from rods, reels, knots, casting, rigging, reading a stream, fly presentation, and of course, hooking, landing and playing trout, all in a way that won't make your head spin. If you stick with us and make it through the first few chapters on equipment, you'll not only master the basics but also save money by selecting the right gear from the start.

Along the way, you'll develop your own style, favorite techniques, and go-to fishing spots. Maybe you'll become obsessed with catching trout in mountain streams. Maybe you'll take your skills to the saltwater flats, chasing after bonefish. Or maybe, just maybe, you'll find that standing in a river, casting a line, and watching the water flow by is enough to keep you coming back.

Whatever your reason for picking up this book, we're glad you're here. Welcome to the world of fly fishing—where the learning never stops, the fish always keep us humble, and the best stories are the ones we bring back from the river.

This books principles can be used in a variety of fly fishing situations, but its scope is primarily focused on fishing in trout streams.

Now, let's get started—before the fish hear us coming.

2
The Fly Rod

The Modern Fly Rod—A Masterpiece of Engineering

Alright, class, gather around. Today, we are here to learn about the fly rod—the most essential (and, let's be honest, the coolest) tool in your fly-fishing arsenal.

I have cast literally thousands of rods, from the first fiberglass ones to today's most expensive graphite models. Over the years, I've learned that the right fly rod can make all the difference—not just in catching fish, but in truly experiencing the art of fly fishing.

Breaking Down the Fly Rod: More Than Just a Stick

If you've ever looked at a fly rod and thought, "It's just a stick with some string attached," well, far from it. Back in the day, fly rods were crafted from bamboo—beautiful, classic, and a very soft action. Then came fiberglass, which was a step up but still had the casting speed of a sleepy sloth. Today, though? We have high-modulus graphite rods, lighter, stronger, and engineered with such precision that NASA might as well be designing them.

Modern fly rods aren't just tools; they're an extension of your arm. They allow for greater casting accuracy, efficient energy transfer, and better sensitivity—all crucial elements that make you look like a pro (even if you're still figuring things out). A high quality fly rod in the hands of a skilled fly fisher makes all the difference.

Selection of Fly Rods and Brands

Fly Rod Anatomy: Know Your Weapon

Before you go waving this thing around like a wizard's staff, let's break down the parts:

Blank – The backbone of the rod, made from ultra-light, high-tech graphite.

Grip – The cork handle, shaped for comfort and control. (A well-worn grip tells the story of a fly fisher's journey.)

Reel Seat – Where your reel locks in. Typically made out of an alloy to lock in your reel. Don't be that ex-spin fishermen who turns the rod upside down with the reel on top. On a fly rod the reel sits on the bottom.

Guides – Metal rings that keep your fly line on track. Without these, you'd be in a world of tangled chaos. From the tip top guide to the stripping guide by the cork, every guide has its purpose.

Ferrules – The joints where multi-piece rods fit together.

Pro tip: When putting your fly rod together, ensure the ferrules (the connecting points between rod sections) fit snugly—secure, but not over-tightened. A small dab of rod wax, or even a bit of natural skin oil from the side of your nose, can help the sections slide together more smoothly and hold better.

Most modern fly rods have alignment dots. Start by inserting each section with the dots offset about 90 degrees. Then, twist and push gently until the dots line up and the sections are firmly connected.

If the ferrules are stuck at the end of the day, don't twist or force them apart. Instead, sit down, place the rod behind your knees, grip both sections, and apply slow, steady pressure to pull them apart. This gives you better leverage and reduces the risk of damaging your rod.

Choosing the Right Fly Rod: One Size Doesn't Fit All

Fly rods come in different weights—ranging from a delicate 1-weight to a powerful 15-weight. The weight doesn't refer to how much the rod actually weighs; rather, it corresponds to the size of the fly line it's meant to cast. Think of it as choosing the right tool for the job. Major fly rod manufacturers follow industry standards, ensuring consistency across brands. Most fly rods have their weight designation printed on the butt section, indicating the appropriate fly line to match. This weight rating (e.g., 5wt, 8wt) helps anglers pair their rod with the right line for optimal performance, making it easier to achieve a balanced and efficient cast.

1-3 weight – Small creeks, tiny flies, and gentle presentations. Small Trout and Panfish. (Perfect for sneaky approaches.)

4-6 weight – Most popular for trout fishing.

7-9 weight – Bigger rivers, wind, and the occasional bass or salmon.

10+ weight – Saltwater fishing and fighting fish that can pull you into the next zip code.

Fly Rod Actions: Speed and Precision

Fly rods also come in different "actions," which affect how they bend and cast:

Slow Action – Bends deeply, great for small streams and good for cold water applications and playing fish. For purists who like bamboo or fiberglass rods.

Medium Action – A versatile choice, balancing finesse with power. Best for beginners.

Fast Action – Stiff and powerful, ideal for windy conditions, long casts, dry fly fishing and increased accuracy.

The Travel-Friendly Revolution: Why Four-Piece Rods Rule

Once upon a time, fly rods were one or two pieces—great for performance but terrible for travel. Ever tried fitting a 9-foot rod into a car? It's like wrestling a giraffe into a suitcase. Modern rods break into four pieces, making them easier to carry without sacrificing performance.

Specialty Rods: Going Beyond the Basics

Fiberglass Rods – Slower, fun to cast, and make small fish feel like monsters. There is a current trend of fly fishers returning to the glass rod.

Tenkara Rods – Minimalist rods with no reel, perfect for backpackers and purists.

Spey Rods – Two-handed casting machines, great for big rivers and salmon fishing. Run up to 13 feet in length so consider how you are going to transport before purchasing.

Choosing Your First Fly Rod

So, what rod should you buy? Here's our honest advice:

- Your local fly shop can assist in determining your casting style and what action you would best suit you.
- For trout get an 8.5 foot to 9 ft. 5 or 6-weight, medium to fast action, four-piece rod.

A Final Thoughts on Fly Rods

Invest in a high-quality fly rod—typically spending over $200 is worth it. Premium rods often come with a solid guarantee, so if a part ever breaks like the tip section, you can simply send that particular section in for repair. Major manufacturers stand behind their products, ensuring that you'll have a rod that lasts a lifetime and grows with your skills.

As a former fly shop owner, I highly recommend you visit and support your local fly shop if there is one in your area. They can assist in outfitting you with the perfect gear to get started, and you won't have to rob a bank to start enjoying this wonderful sport. A good shop is more than just a place to buy gear—it's a hub of knowledge, experience, and a community of fly fishers who share your passion. Whether you need advice on fly selection, casting techniques, or just a great fishing story, your local fly shop is the place to start.

Organization is key to success on the way to river

3
The Fly Reel

The Fly Reel: A Silent Workhorse

The fly reel is often overlooked by beginners. But make no mistake—it plays a crucial role in balancing your rod, managing your line, and, most importantly, helping you fight the fish of a lifetime.

Machined vs. Stamped Fly Reels: What's the Difference?

When choosing a fly reel, one key distinction is whether it's machined or stamped. Machined reels are precision-cut from solid bar stock aluminum, making them lighter, stronger, and more durable—ideal for serious anglers who demand longevity and performance. Stamped reels, on the other hand, are made by pressing metal into shape, often resulting in a more affordable option but with added weight and less durability. While stamped reels can work well for beginners or casual anglers, machined reels offer superior craftsmanship and longevity, making them a worthwhile investment for those dedicated to the sport.

Why Machined Reels are Great:

- Smooth with a wide range of torque.
- Lightweight and incredibly durable.
- Built with precision to ensure smooth operation.
- Holds up against wear and tear, making it a long-term investment.
- Price: $200 to $800+. Quality comes at a cost, but it's worth it.

Why You Might Regret a Stamped Reel:

- More fragile—one hard drop, and it may bend or break.
- Weak drag system—not built for fighting powerful fish.
- Corrosion-prone—especially in saltwater environments.

Verdict: If you're serious about fly fishing, go with a machined reel. If you're just getting started, a stamped reel will do, but don't expect it to last forever.

The Drag System: Mastering the Fight

When a trout makes a run you don't muscle it in. You let the drag do the work while leading fish away from trouble with the rod tip.

Disc Drag (What Most Modern Reels Use):

- Uses carbon, cork, or ceramic discs to provide adjustable friction.
- Allows for smooth, controlled resistance when fighting bigger fish.
- Sealed versions keep out dirt and water, extending reel life.

The Downside: Costs more, but if you plan to chase anything stronger than a bluegill, it's worth every penny.

Large Arbor Reels: Speed and Efficiency

Years ago, reels had tiny spools, which meant you had to reel like mad just to bring in your line. Then came the large arbor reel.

Why Large Arbor Reels Are the Standard Today:

- Faster line pickup – 3:1 to 4:1 pickup. Less cranking, more fishing.
- Reduces fly line memory – No more coiled, curly fly line disasters.
- Better drag performance – More surface area means smoother drag.

Match Your Reel to Your Rod Weight:

- 5-weight rod? Get a 5-weight reel.
- Avoid mismatched setups, or your casting will feel awkward.

Freshwater vs. Saltwater Reels:

- Saltwater reels must be anodized and have a sealed drag system.
- Freshwater reels are more affordable but still require proper maintenance.

Where to Invest Your Money:

A high end rod and fly line will improve your casting more than a high-end reel. Your rod and reel are in your hands on every cast, but while your rod is in constant use, your reel plays a more situational role. You rely on it when fighting a fish, recovering line from a snag, or adjusting your setup between casts, changing rigs, or moving to a new location. A quality reel may not be engaged on every cast, but when the moment comes, it needs to perform flawlessly. If on a budget, get a mid-range reel and spend extra on a better fly rod and line.

If You're Fishing Big Fish, Invest in Drag

Small trout? A basic drag system is fine. Chasing big-game fish? Get the best drag system you can afford.

Fly Reels as Functional Art

Beyond function, fly reels have also become collector's items, with companies like Abel and Ross Reels crafting custom anodized reels featuring trout patterns, tarpon scales, personalized artwork, and limited-edition conservation themes with laser-engraved wildlife designs. Are these reels necessary? Not at all. But are they ridiculously cool? Absolutely. Sometimes, fly fishing isn't just about function—it's about passion, craftsmanship, and a little bit of art.

Fly Line Backing: The Unsung Hero of Your Reel

Your fly line is only about 90-100 feet long.

Backing:

- Fills the spool for better retrieval rates.
- Prevents fly line coil memory.
- Improves reel balance.
- Provides extra insurance for long fights.
- Prevents you from running out of line when a fish makes a long run.

How Much Backing Do You Need?

- 3-5 weight reels: 50-100 yards
- 6-8 weight reels: 100-200 yards
- 9+ weight reels: 200-300+ yards

Final Thoughts on Fly Reels and Backing

When purchasing a new reel, it's best to visit your local fly shop and have them spool the backing for you. They'll ensure the correct amount, tension, and right knots are used, so you don't run into problems on the water.

Vail Valley Anglers Fly Shop – Edwards, Colorado

4
The Fly Line

Fly Lines: The Engine of Your Cast

Now, let's talk about fly lines. You might think your rod and reel are the stars of the show, but without the right fly line, you'd be flinging fluff into the wind with no direction, power, or purpose.

Unlike traditional fishing, where the lure's weight does all the work, fly fishing relies on the weight of the fly line to carry the fly to its target. Choosing the right fly line is just as important as picking the right rod or reel.

Fly Line Weight: Match It or Struggle Forever

The American Fly-Fishing Trade Association (AFFTA) standardized fly line weights from 1-weight (ultra-light) to 15-weight (big-game heavy-duty).

A 5-weight line is the most versatile for freshwater trout fishing. Match your rod to your fly line or you'll be fighting your gear instead of the fish.

Fly Line Colors: Is It a Fashion Statement?

You'll see fly lines in every color, from pale green to screaming neon orange. But does it actually matter?

Muted Colors (Grey, Olive, Pale Blue): Great for clear water where subtlety helps avoid spooking fish.

Bright Colors (Fluorescent Orange, Yellow, Chartreuse): Easier to see and track for beginners, especially in fast-moving water or low light.

Does color spook fish?

It can, but not necessarily. It might be an issue if targeting trophy fish in ultra clear waters of New Zealand or Western Spring Creeks. If you're using the right leader and tippet, the fish won't even see your fly line. Bad presentation spooks more fish rather than you fly line color.

Decoding Fly Line Labels

Ever stare at a wall of fly lines in the shop and wonder what all those codes mean? Here's what you need to know.

Code	Meaning
WF	Weight Forward (the most common type)
6	Line Weight (must match your rod)
F	Floating Line

WF = Weight Forward (most common and easiest to cast).

DT = Double Taper. If one end of the line gets worn, simply reverse it and you have a new line.

6 = The line weight (must match your rod weight).

F = Floating line (the best choice for beginners and trout fishing).

For most of you a WF/F (Weight Forward Floating) line is the best place to start.

Fly Line Tapers: The Science of Casting

A fly line taper affects how the energy transfers through your cast and how the fly lands.

Weight Forward (WF): Best for beginners—easier to cast.

Double Taper (DT): Great for delicate presentations.

Shooting Taper (ST): Built for distance casting.

Verdict: WF is the best choice for most anglers because it makes casting easier.

Floating vs. Sinking Fly Lines: What's the Deal?

Fly lines aren't just about weight and color. Some float; some sink.

Floating lines (F): Best for dry flies and general trout fishing.

Sink-tip lines: The front sinks while the rest floats—great for getting flies deeper, especially for streamers.

Full-sinking lines: Ideal for deep-water fishing. Mostly used in lakes.

If you're fishing for trout stick with a floating line. If you're going deep, that's when sinking lines come into play. Most reels allow you to swap out spools, so you can easily switch line types if needed.

Specialty Fly Lines: Do You Need a Custom Line?

Today's fly lines are designed for specific species and conditions. Here are a few specialty options.

Coldwater Lines: Stay flexible in freezing temperatures.

Tropical Lines: Stiffer, so they don't turn limp in the heat.

Nymphing Lines: Ultra-thin for better sensitivity.

Do you need these? Maybe. But for now, stick with a standard floating line until you figure out your style. You will typically be selecting a trout line when you first start out.

Caring for Your Fly Line: Keep It Casting Smoothly

Your fly line collects dirt, algae, and grime over time. A dirty line won't float and makes casting harder. Keep it clean.

- Use a fly line cleaner to remove buildup. A dirty fly line can stick in your guides and make it difficult to cast. Typically, this is only 30 to 40 feet of your line. Commercial fly line cleaners are available; however, soap and water works fine.
- Store out of direct sun & extreme heat to prevent damage.

By matching your fly line to your fishing needs, you'll improve your casting, presentation, and overall success on the water.

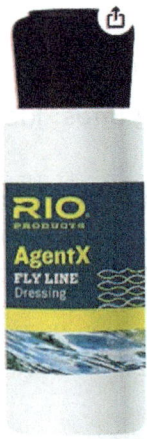

5
Knots

If you're waiting until you're on the water to practice tying knots, you're already making one of the biggest mistakes in fly fishing. By reading this book you can become a pro at tying knots with about 15 minutes of practice.

There's nothing worse than standing next to the river, fish rising in front of you, and instead of casting, you're fumbling with a knot that just won't cinch down. So here is a pro tip—practice these knots at home. Learn them so well you can tie them in your sleep. Because when the fish are feeding, you don't want to be stuck on river bank fighting with your tippet. Learning and perfecting knot tying is also available via the internet on YouTube videos.

The 3 Essential Knots You'll Use 95% of the Time

If you only learn a few knots, make them these. They'll cover almost every situation you'll run into on the water.

- Improved Clinch Knot (Fishermen's Knot) – Attaches the fly to the tippet.
- Surgeon's Knot – Connects tippet to leader.
- Loop-to-Loop Connection – The fastest and strongest way to connect your leader to your fly line.

Why these knots? Because they're quick, strong, and reliable under pressure. If you can tie them cleanly and fast, you'll spend more time fishing and less time re-rigging. And trust me, the fish don't wait for you to get your act together.

Step-by-Step Instructions for Essential Fly-Fishing Knots

When you practice at home, use two different colors of string as it makes it easier to see what's happening. And don't just practice once or twice—tie these knots until they feel as natural as casting. Your future self on the river will thank you.

The Improved Clinch Knot (A.K.A. Fishermen's Knot)

Photos Courtesy of Norrik Fishing (www.norrick.com)

This is your go-to knot for securing flies to your tippet—whether you're casting dry flies, nymphs, or small streamers. No fancy loops here—just a strong, direct connection for maximum control, especially in fast-moving water. This knot holds at about 98% of your line strength.

How to Tie It:

1. Thread the Line – Pass the tag end through the hook eye and pull 6-8 inches of line to work with.
2. Wrap It Up – Wrap the tag end 5-7 times around the standing line—keep it neat!
3. Thread It Through – Insert the tag end through the small loop near the hook eye.
4. Make the Final Loop – Pass the tag end back through the larger loop you just created.
5. Tighten Up – Moisten the knot (yes, spit works!), then pull the standing line to cinch it tight.
6. Trim the Excess – Snip the tag end close, but not too close—a tiny bit of extra line is your insurance policy.

Pro tip: Learn this one first—it'll be your workhorse knot out on the river.

The Double Surgeon's Knot (For connecting similar diameter line)

Quickest way to connect tippet to leader. That's where the Surgeon's Knot comes in. It's fast, strong, and a must for nymphing rigs or tippet extensions. The only drawback is that as you add more wraps, the knot becomes larger, which can sometimes be noticeable in your tippet and may cause slight drag in the water.

How to Tie It:

1. Lay the Lines Together – Overlap the two lines by several inches.
2. Make a Simple Loop – Tie a loose overhand knot with both lines, leaving a loop.
3. Pass Through Again – Take both tag ends and pass them through the loop a second time.
4. Tighten the Knot – Moisten it, then pull all four ends to cinch it tight.
5. Trim Extra Line – Snip the excess tag ends close to the knot.

This knot keeps your connections smooth, meaning your line won't catch on your guides as you cast. The fewer snags, the better.

Loop to Loop Connection (For connecting dissimilar diameter line)

The loop-to-loop connection is one of the simplest and most effective ways to attach your leader to your fly line or to connect two sections of a leader together quickly. This connection allows for easy rig changes, maintains strength, and won't compromise your casting.

It's a friction-based connection, and when done correctly, it locks securely while still being easy to undo when you need to swap out a leader.

How to Tie It:

1. Form the Loops – Your fly line should already have a welded loop. If your leader does not, tie a perfection loop at the end.
2. Interlock the Loops – Pass the leader's loop through the fly line's loop.
3. Thread the Leader Through – Take the long end of the leader and pass it completely through its own loop.
4. Tighten the Connection – Pull both the fly line and the leader in opposite directions to snug the loops together.
5. Check Your Work – The loops should seat neatly against each other without crossing or twisting.

Time to level up your knot game. Now, we're covering essential connection knots for attaching leaders, tippets, backing, and more.

The Blood Knot (For Seamless Line Connections)

If you want a strong, smooth connection between two lines of similar diameter—especially when building custom leaders—the Blood Knot is your best bet. It creates a low-profile connection that slides through your guides effortlessly, making it perfect for situations where you want a seamless transition in your line.

This knot might take a little more practice than the Surgeon's Knot, but once you get it down, it's one of the strongest and cleanest knots you can tie.

How to Tie It:

1. Overlap the Lines – Place both lines end-to-end, overlapping about 6-8 inches.
2. Wrap the First Line – Take one tag end and wrap it 5-7 times around the other line, then tuck the tag through the small gap in the middle where the lines overlap.
3. Wrap the Second Line – Repeat the same process with the other tag end, wrapping it in the opposite direction and tucking it back through the center.
4. Tighten the Knot – Moisten the knot, then slowly pull both main lines evenly to cinch it down.
5. Trim Excess – Snip the tag ends close to the knot for a clean, streamlined connection.

Make sure you have an equal number of wraps on both sides to maximize strength. A lopsided Blood Knot is a weak Blood Knot.

This is one of the most useful knots in fly fishing. If you're building your own leaders or need a strong connection that won't snag or slip, this is the knot to use.

Now we're moving on to one of the most important knots for attaching backing to your reel.

The Nail Knot (For Attaching Leader to Fly Line)

When you need to attach a leader to a fly line without a loop-to-loop connection, the Nail Knot is the best option. It creates a strong, seamless connection that slides smoothly through the guides of your rod.

You can use a nail knot tying tool made specifically for this knot.

How to Tie It:

1. Align the Fly Line & Leader – Place them parallel, overlapping about 6 inches.
2. Use a Nail or Tube – Lay a small tube (or actual nail) along the overlap as a guide.
3. Wrap the Leader – Wrap the tag end around both the fly line and itself 5-7 times.
4. Thread the Tag End – Pass it through the center of the wraps (where the nail was), then slide the nail out.
5. Tighten the Knot – Moisten the wraps, then pull both ends of the leader to snug it up securely.
6. Trim Excess – Snip the tag ends for a clean finish.

A well-tied Nail Knot is strong, streamlined, and won't snag on your rod guides. If you want extra security, add a drop of super glue or UV resin. That will keep everything locked in place.

This is an essential knot if your fly line doesn't have a welded loop. Once you master it, you'll always have a way to attach a leader quickly and efficiently to your fly line.

Practice. Practice. Practice. Knots aren't the most exciting part of fly fishing, but they're one of the most important. The better you are at tying them, the more time you'll spend fishing instead of rigging. So, practice now—before you're on the water, before the fish are rising or before you're fumbling under pressure.

BUILDING A BOND BETWEEN FATHER AND SON

6
Terminal Tackle

Now we're going to discuss leaders and tippet—the essential piece of your fly-fishing setup. Without them, you'd be spooking fish left and right, and you'd be tying your fly straight to your thick fly line, which would be a disaster.

What a Leader Does

A leader is a tapered, clear section of line, made from monofilament or fluorocarbon, that connects your fly line to your fly. It's the bridge between your cast and a perfect drift, helping your fly land naturally without a splashy entrance.

Leader Structure: The Three Key Parts

Every leader has three key parts. Each plays a role in delivering your fly exactly where you want it.

Butt Section (Thickest Part, ~60%) – Transfers energy from the fly line for smooth casting.

Tapered Section (Midsection, ~20%) – Gradually decreases in diameter for control.

Tippet Section (Thinnest Part, ~20%) – The delicate section where your fly attaches—or where you add more tippet.

Types of Leaders

There's a leader for every situation. Let's go over your options.

Knotless Tapered Leaders (Most Common Choice!)

- Made from a single piece of material with a smooth taper.
- Provides seamless energy transfer (aka: better casting).
- Comes in lengths of 7.5 ft, 9 ft, 12 ft, and 15 ft.

Hand-Tied Leaders (For the DIY Angler)
- Made by tying different diameters of line together.
- Customizable for specific fishing conditions.
- Downside: Knots can collect algae & debris.
- Takes more time to create using a series of blood knots.

Without a leader, your fly line would land like a rock on the water, scaring everything away. A properly matched leader helps deliver your fly naturally and increases hookups.

Choosing the Right Leader

Selecting the right leader for fly fishing is much like choosing the perfect dance partner—each step must flow smoothly to create a graceful performance. The leader is the critical connection between your fly line and the fly itself, and choosing correctly can make all the difference between an elegant cast and one that scares the trout away.

Where Are You Fishing?

If you're fishing on a lake or in still water, longer leaders (9 to 12 feet) are ideal. The calm surface means fish have more time to inspect the fly, so a delicate, natural presentation is crucial. Fluorocarbon leaders are often the best choice in lakes because they sink slightly and are nearly invisible underwater, helping to present nymphs and streamers more naturally.

In a river, shorter leaders (7.5 to 9 feet) provide better control and accuracy in moving water. Fast currents require quick adjustments, and shorter leaders help transfer energy from the cast more effectively. Monofilament leaders tend to work well in rivers since they float better and are easier to manage when dry fly fishing.

Matching Leader to Fly Type and Size

The type and size of fly you plan to cast also determine the best leader choice:

- **Small dry flies** (sizes 18 to 24): Use a longer, thinner leader (5X to 6X) to create a delicate, natural drift.
- **Larger dry flies** (sizes 10 to 16): A medium-length leader (9 to 12 feet) with a 4X or 5X rating balances strength and finesse.
- **Nymphs**: Use fluorocarbon leaders, as they sink and present nymphs naturally. Go shorter (7.5 to 9 feet) with 4X to 6X for improved strike detection.
- **Streamers**: Heavier streamers require a shorter, thicker leader (3X or even 0X) for turnover and control. A shorter leader (7.5 feet) gives you better accuracy and handling.

Final Thought

Choosing the right leader isn't about complexity—it's about understanding where you're fishing, what you're fishing with, and how to present the fly naturally. With the right leader, your fly will drift effortlessly, fooling even the wisest trout.

Always Carry an Extra Leader

Your leader is critical to a good presentation, and it can wear out, break, or get tangled at the worst times. Always carry a backup leader so you're not left struggling on the water.

Choosing the Right Tippet

Now, let's talk about tippet—the workhorse of your rig. Think of it as the sacrificial section that lets you change flies without shortening your leader. For smaller dry flies and nymphs, go with finer tippet (5X to 6X) to create a more natural drift. For larger flies and streamers, thicker tippet (0X to 3X) helps transfer casting energy and handle aggressive strikes.

Why Tippet Rocks

- Much more supple than a leader and it's why we use it at the end.
- Invisible Connection – Keeps your fly stealthy.
- Lifelike Presentation – Helps your fly drift naturally.
- Leader Longevity – Saves your leader from constant trimming.
- Shock Absorption – Cushions the fight against strong fish.

Tippet Materials: Mono vs. Fluorocarbon

Each type has it's uses, pros and cons.

Monofilament (Nylon)

- Floats – Best for dry flies.
- Stretchy – Reduces break-offs.
- Less Abrasion-Resistant – Wears out faster on rocks and structure.

Fluorocarbon

- Sinks – Perfect for nymphs & streamers.
- Tough as Nails – Handles rocks & toothy fish.
- Stealth Mode – Nearly invisible underwater.
- More Expensive – Usually 3x the cost of mono.

The X-System: Cracking the Code

Forget pound test—fly fishing uses an X-rating system (but keep your mind on this book) to measure tippet thickness.

Here's how it works.

- Smaller X = Thicker, Stronger Tippet (0X for big streamers)
- Larger X = Thinner, More Delicate Tippet (7X for tiny dry flies)

Pro tip: Carry multiple tippet spool in different sizes to match your fly. That way, you'll get better presentations, fewer break-offs, and more fish in the net. If you purchase tippet spools from the same manufacturer they attach

Tippet Size

Tippet Size	Diameter (inches)	Pound Test	Fly Size Range
0X	.011	15-18 lb	2-6
1X	.010	13-16 lb	4-8
2X	.009	11-13 lb	6-10
3X	.008	8-10 lb	10-14
4X	.007	6-8 lb	12-16
5X	.006	4-6 lb	14-18
6X	.005	3-4 lb	16-22
7X	.004	2-3 lb	20-28
8X	.003	1-2 lb	24-32

Tippet Sizing Made Easy

Here's a simple formula to match your tippet to your fly size.

Fly Size ÷ 3 = Tippet Size

Example: A size 12 fly → 12 ÷ 3 = 4X tippet. Simple, right?

This little formula will save you time and make sure you're using the right tippet for the job.

Tippet Rings: The Secret to Long-Lasting Leaders

Tippet rings make changing tippet easy and extend the life of your leader. Instead of cutting and retying your leader every time, you simply swap out the tippet—saving time and material.

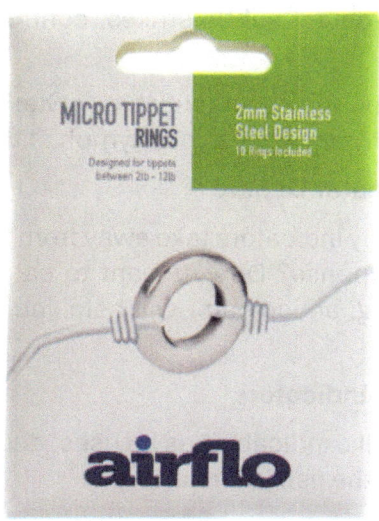

Why Use Them?

✓ Saves Leader Material – No need to cut your leader when replacing tippet. ✓ Faster Rigging – Change tippet sizes in seconds. ✓ Great for Pre-Rigging – Prepare multiple leader setups in advance. ✓ Reduces Waste – Less trimming means more fishing. ✓ Provides a nice hinge point – Less drag. ✓ Works for All Rigs – Perfect for nymphing, streamers, and even dry flies.

How to Use Them

- Attach your leader to the ring with an Improved Clinch Knot.
- Tie your tippet to the ring the same way.
- Add your fly and start fishing!

With tippet rings, you'll spend more time fishing and less time retying.

Strike Indicators in Fly Fishing: A Complete Guide

Some fly purist's frown on strike indicators, but if you want to catch more fish while nymphing, an indicator is your best friend. It helps detect subtle strikes, control depth, and improve your drift.

Think of it as a bobber—but fly-fishing style! It signals when a fish takes your fly and keeps your nymph at the right depth.

The Great Indicator Debate

Some anglers say indicators take away from the 'true art' of fly fishing. Our response? Do you want to catch fish or not? If you're nymphing, an indicator will help you catch more fish. Period.

Types of Strike Indicators

Each type of strike indicator has its uses, depending on water conditions and the fish you're after.

- Foam and Plastic Indicators (Air-Lock, Thingamabobber). These float the best. Newer versions use biodegradable designs.
- Stick-On Indicators (Convenient)
- Yarn & Wool Indicators. (Stealthy presentations)
- Peg Type Indicators. Good for still-water.

Pro Tip: Give your yarn indicator a lift—literally! Use the Velcro on your fly vest to fluff the fibers. This helps it float better and keeps your fly at the perfect depth.

Setting Indicator Depth for Maximum Success

A properly adjusted indicator ensures your flies drift naturally in the feeding zone. Here's the rule of thumb:

Set the indicator 1.5 to 2 times the water depth.

Example: Fishing 3 feet of water? Place the indicator 4.5 - 6 feet from the fly.

Pro Tip: Indicators come is various sizes. Mastering indicator depth and setup will boost your hookup rate and make you a better nymph angler. Adjust, experiment, and start landing more fish.

Best Colors for Different Conditions

Orange, Pink, Yellow or Chartreuse – Provide high visibility.

Clear, White or Neutral Tones – Best for spooky fish in calm water.

Types of Weights for Fly Fishing: Choosing the Right Option

Now, we're talking weights—the unsung heroes of nymph fishing. Whether you need to sink your flies deep or fine-tune your drift, picking the right weight makes all the difference.

Lead Split Shot (Classic but Controversial)

- Soft, easy to crimp, and affordable.
- Comes in multiple sizes (BB, AAA, #6, #8, etc.).
- Toxic—banned in some states.
- Never bite it! Use pliers to avoid poisoning yourself.

Tin Weights: Fly fishing tin weights are an eco-friendly alternative to traditional lead split shot, designed to help anglers achieve the perfect depth while nymphing or fishing subsurface patterns. Made from non-toxic tin, these weights are safer for the environment, particularly in waterways where lead can be harmful to fish and wildlife. Available in various sizes and shapes, tin weights provide excellent versatility, allowing anglers to fine-tune their presentations without damaging their leader. Easy to pinch on and remove, they offer a reusable and responsible solution for weighting flies while maintaining a delicate and natural drift. Tin weights come in earth tones like brown and green. Always use nippers to pinch on and off.

Tungsten Putty

- Sinks faster than lead with less bulk.
- Moldable—just pinch on or take off.
- No splashdown—great for spooky fish.
- Can slide down the leader if not applied correctly.

Best Use: Fine-tuning weight on delicate rigs, but honestly, we prefer a bead-head fly instead.

Always Carry a Split Shot Selector

Conditions change, and different rivers need different weights. Instead of buying one size, get a selector pack so you can adjust on the fly.

What About Lead Strips?

Once popular, but they kink leaders and cause tangles. Now, they're better for fly tying than for weighting rigs.

Pro Tip: Nowadays, many anglers find that using a couple of tungsten-weighted type flies is easier and more effective than using split shot. This modern approach offers a streamlined method that can simplify your rig setup while providing a more snag free approach as the hooks sits upright.

Fly Floatant: Keeping Your Dry Flies Riding High

Fly floatant—your best friend when keeping dry flies riding high and natural. But here's the catch: floatant alone won't do the trick! Line speed, clean casting, and the right floatant mix all play a role.

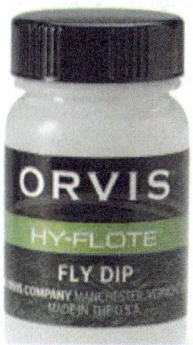  

Gel Floatant (Pre-Fishing Treatment)

Best for initial fly treatment before hitting the water.

Rub a small amount into the hackle and body with your fingers for a water-repellent barrier and blow on the fly to dry.

Perfect for big, bushy dries.

Downside: Hardens in cold weather and gets runny in hot weather.

Pro Tip: Store gel upside down in a vest caddy for quick access.

Dry Shake (Desiccant Revives a Waterlogged Fly!)

Best for post-fish or soggy flies—absorbs moisture fast. Restores buoyancy instantly—perfect for when a fly gets slimy.

Doesn't replace initial gel floatant.

Liquid Floatant

Dunk & dry method—treats the whole fly.

Great for pre-treatment the night before.

Needs drying time before fishing and can leave a shiny residue. Application can also be messy to work with.

Pro Tip: Blot the fly first with a Handy Map Microfiber Cloth before using dry shake, then apply desiccant—then blow on and apply your gel floatant again. Purchase at www.mapthexperience.com

Common Mistake: Using dry shake as a first coat!

Correct Order:
1. Gel Floatant → Fish the Fly
2. Blot Dry with a Microfiber Cloth
3. Use Desiccant Powder
4. Apply Gel Floatant Again

A dry fly that stays on top catches more trout. Use gel, dip, and powder strategically to keep your flies floating longer and looking natural. Now go out and keep those dries riding high!

7
Fly Rod Rigging

Mastering Fly Rod Rigging

Now it's time to get rigged up. A properly rigged fly rod is the foundation of a successful day on the water. Whether you're drifting dries, swinging streamers, or nymphing deep, a well-balanced setup makes casting smoother, presentations cleaner, and hookups more frequent. Let's break down the most common fly-fishing rigs and how to set them up like a pro.

Single Dry Fly Rig (The Classic Setup)

Fly Line: Weight-forward floating line.
Leader: 7.5 to 9 ft monofilament leader (match size to fly).
Tippet: 4X-6X (lighter tippet = better drift, but less strength).
Fly: Dry fly (match the hatch!).
Floatant: Apply gel before fishing.

Setup Steps: Let's rig up a single dry fly setup the right way. This setup is all about stealth, accuracy, and keeping that fly riding high on the surface. Follow these steps for the perfect presentation.

Adjust Leader & Tippet Length

- Clear, slow water? Go long (12 ft) for a stealthier approach.
- Fast, deep water? Stick to 7.5-9 ft for better turnover.

Pro Tips:

- Use monofilament leader for dry flies—it floats better than fluorocarbon!
- Always carry multiple tippet sizes. Smaller flies = thinner tippet!

- Keep your tippet fresh: If it gets abrasions or too short from fly changes, add 12-24 inches of tippet using a double surgeon's or blood knot.
- If you want to fish two dries, separate the flies by 24 inches, step down at least one size in tippet and use the smaller fly as the back one.

Dry Dropper Rig: The Best of Both Worlds!

Let's talk about one of the most effective setups you can use—the Dry Dropper Rig. There are a number of different ways to do it.

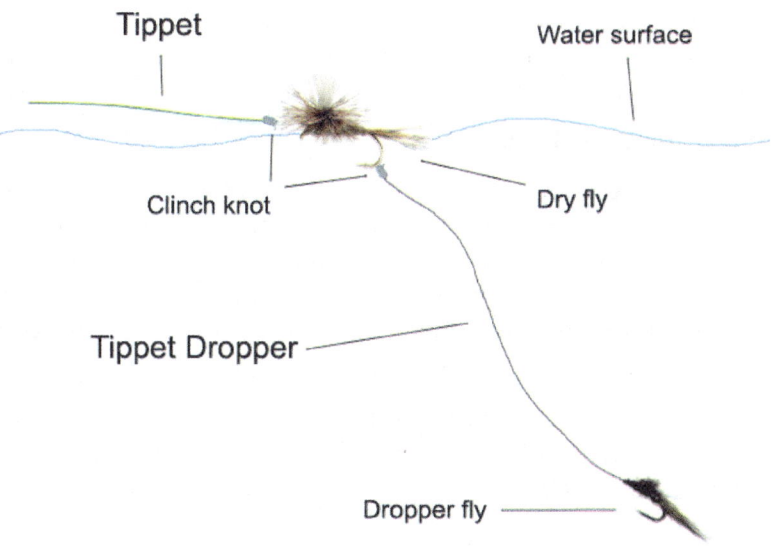

Photos Courtesy of Norrik.com

First things first—you need a dry fly that stays afloat. If your dry fly sinks, it's game over for this setup. You're looking for something buoyant, like a Chubby Chernobyl. If your fly keeps getting pulled under, either switch to a more buoyant pattern, go up a size, or reduce the weight of your dropper nymph.

Tie on the Dropper

Use anywhere from 12 to 24 inches of tippet depending on how deep you want the nymph to drift tied either to the leader tippet or to the dry fly.

Some of you might be wondering, 'Can I use three flies?' In some states, absolutely—but check the regulations before you rig up.

Select the Right Dropper Nymph

If your dropper is pulling your dry fly under, it's time to change your nymph. Try a lighter pattern, switch to a smaller bead size, or use a slower-sinking fly to maintain a natural drift without sinking your dry.

Fine-Tune Your Setup

Here's where a lot of beginning fly fishers can go wrong. The tippet length determines how deep that nymph rides, so don't be afraid to adjust if you're not getting bites. And always—always—check your dry fly. If it starts sinking, it could be that it is tangled, so check that first. If it is not tangled dry it off with microfiber cloth, apply desiccant, and reapply floatant.

Pro tip: Remember, set the hook at any sign of movement. Sometimes the dry fly just twitches—that could be a fish taking the nymph below.

Double Nymph Rig: Twice the Flies, Twice the Chances!

Double Nymph Rig Setup

Photos Courtesy of Norrik.com

Who wants to double their chances of hooking fish?

That's exactly what a Double Nymph Rig does. By fishing two different nymphs at different depths, you cover more of the water column, increasing your odds of finding what the fish are eating and where.

Pick Your Nymphs Wisely

Now, you can't just throw on any two flies and expect magic. Consider these combos:

Big & Small – A larger attractor nymph, like a stonefly, with a smaller imitative nymph, like a Pheasant Tail.

Heavy & Light – A tungsten bead nymph to get deep fast, paired with a lighter emerger for mid-depth action.

Drift & Drop – A weighted nymph to sink the rig, with an unweighted fly for a natural, tumbling drift.

Pro tip: If fish are feeding near the bottom, your heavier fly should be on the bottom. If they're mid-column, reverse it.

Rigging the Double Nymph Setup

One option is to tie 12-24 inches of tippet to the smaller hook's bend, then attach a larger fly so it bounces along the bottom.

You can also use a loop and bring the fly through the loop and attach above the larger bottom fly, thus creating an emerger effect.

Why do you think this works so well?

Because it keeps the flies in different parts of the water column. You're giving trout options.

Finding the Right Depth: Fish Aren't Always on the Bottom

Fish could be hugging the bottom early in the day. Typically, they'll feed deep until insects start hatching, then move up in the water column. As the hatch progresses, you might need to adjust your flies, fly set up, weights, or indicators to stay in the strike zone.

Drift, Adjust, & Set the Hook!

Now comes the fun part—fly fishing. You need a long, drag-free drift. Mend the line to keep the flies moving naturally.

If you're not getting bites, adjust your depth. Move the indicator up or down until you find the fish. And here's the big one—set the hook on every hesitation or pause. Trout take nymphs subtly, so don't wait for a big yank! We recommend lifting and setting at least once per drift. If you do pull and you feel nothing, then let the line drift downstream to where you can make another cast using the currents tension on the line to load it, then simply cast your rod forward aiming the rod tip where you want the fly to land.

Now, let's talk about two powerhouse techniques, Czech nymphing and streamer fishing. Master these, and you'll start catching fish where others struggle.

Czech Nymphing Rig: Tight-Line Tactics for Fast Water

This method comes from Eastern Europe and is deadly effective in fast-moving streams. It keeps your flies bouncing along the bottom, right where the trout are feeding. And best of all—no indicator.

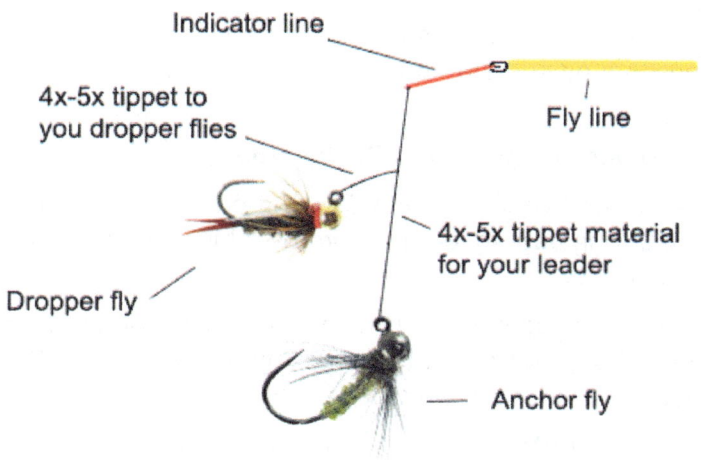

Key Components of a Czech Nymph Rig

Leader: 10-15 ft tapered leader with a bright sighter section—this acts as your strike detector.

Flies: Two or three weighted nymphs, with a heavy anchor fly on the bottom to get the rig down fast. Jig hooks work great.

No Indicator: Your sighter is your visual cue—watch it for twitches, hesitations, or unnatural movement.

Short Line, Tight Control: Keep the rod high and eliminate slack—this keeps you in direct contact with the flies.

Using your Rod Tip: Follow the line.

Unlike traditional casting, Czech nymphing is about short drifts. You're standing close to the target water, leading your flies with your rod tip. The goal? Imitate drifting nymphs—without drag.

This technique is best used in riffles, drop offs, deep runs, and fast currents where indicators struggle. Master this method, and you'll hook fish that everyone else misses.

Streamer Rig: Big Flies, Big Fish!

Now, if Czech nymphing is about finesse, streamer fishing is about aggression. Big flies mean big fish.

Streamers mimic baitfish, leeches, and other large prey—things that aggressive trout and especially big browns love to attack.

How to Set Up a Streamer Rig for Trout

Short, Strong Leader: Use a 0X–2X monofilament leader (or just a strong butt section) to turn over big flies with a fluorocarbon tippet.

Attach the Streamer: Tie it with a non-slip loop knot (like a Duncan Loop or Uni Knot) for maximum movement. *Search YouTube for video on tying these knots.*

Add Weight (If Needed): Use conehead, bead head, or tungsten-weighted streamers to get deep without split shot.

Double Trouble (Optional Second Streamer): Tie a second streamer 18-24 inches behind the first, attached to the hook bend.

Pro tip—Your first fly could be flashy or brightly colored to grab attention and makes it easier to spot.

The second fly? Might be more lifelike or articulated which is the fly trout often eat.

8
Fly Casting

Perfecting the Cast

Before we hit the river, we practice. Why? Because once you're on the water, things change. Your nerves get in the way. There's current, trees, and fish to think about. Out there, it's just you and your rod. Fly casting is easy to learn but difficult to master.

Safety Tip: If you are beginner fly caster and plan on practicing, it is best to make sure that you keep the rod tip offset and away from your head, wear a cap and glasses, and use a fly without a hook or even a small piece of yarn.

Line Hand and Rod Hand

In fly casting, you have two key hands at work:

Rod Hand – This is your dominant hand, which holds the fly rod and controls the cast. It sets the pace, angle, and power of your forward and back cast.

Line Hand – Your non-dominant hand, which manages the fly line. It controls the amount of line you're feeding out or stripping in, helps maintain tension during the cast, and is key to setting the hook and playing the fish.

Coordinating the two hands can feel a bit like rubbing your belly and patting your head at first—but once you find the rhythm, it becomes second nature and makes your casting smoother and more effective.

The Proper Grip: Where It All Starts

The proper grip:

✓ **Thumb on Top** – Your thumb is your guide. Keep it on top of the handle to direct your cast.

✓ **Relaxed Grip** – Squeeze too tight, and you kill your cast. Too loose, and you lose control.

✓ **The Sam Snead Rule** – Hold the rod like you would a small bird—firm enough that it won't escape, but gentle enough that you won't crush it.

✓ **Body Alignment** – A well-balanced ¾ stance is best, allowing you to keep an eye on both your forward and back cast. Your weight should be evenly distributed with an athletic posture—a slight bend in the knees and your dominant foot slightly back to improve balance and stability.

The right grip is the foundation of everything. Get this wrong, and the rest won't matter.

✓ **Single Finger Grip** – Some women, children or people with smaller hands find it helpful to place an index finger on top of the grip.

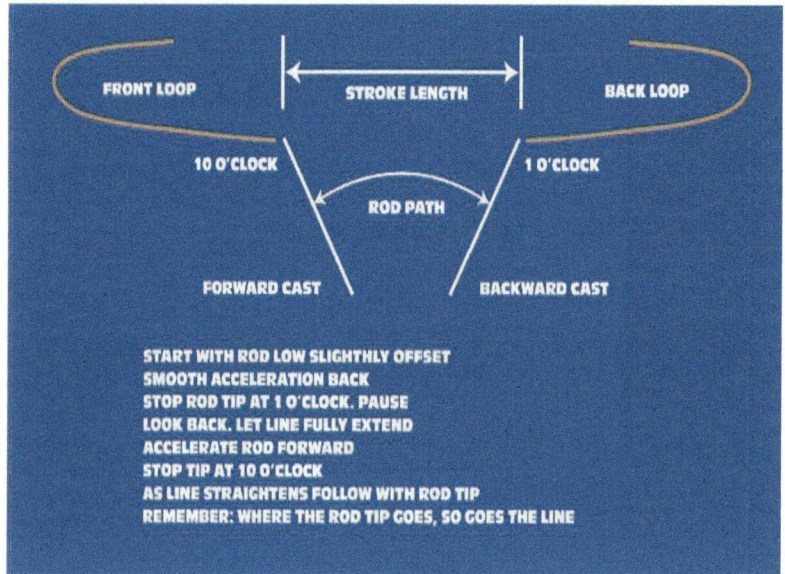

Step 1: The Back Cast

✓ **Start Low** – Keep your rod tip low, pointing slightly downward toward your target and slightly offset

✓ **Smooth Acceleration** – Don't jerk it back. A smooth acceleration is key.

✓ **Stop at 1 O'clock** – Your rod and tip should stop here, with a tight loop unrolling behind you.

✓ **Watch Your Line** – Most beginners struggle because they don't watch their back cast.

✓ **Pause Briefly** – Let the line fully extend before moving into the forward cast.

The Forward Cast

Accelerate & Stop – Accelerate your rod forward when your line has fully extended on the back cast behind you, do not let the line hit the ground. Once the line has fully extended you bring your rod forward in a crisp, fluid motion stopping at 10 o'clock—this sends the line forward.

✓ Follow Through – Lower the rod tip as the fly lands gently.
✓ Remember: The line follows the rod tip. Where your tip goes, your fly follows!

✓ Slightly offset your rod so you do not cast into the back of your head.

Timing & Power Control

✓ Wait for the Line to Straighten – Rushing leads to a collapsed cast.
✓ Accelerate Smoothly – Power comes from the rod tip, not brute force.
✓ Crisp Stop – Stopping the rod abruptly at 1 o'clock and 10 o'clock transfers energy into the line, forming a tight loop.

Common Overhead Cast Mistakes & Fixes

Too Much Wrist Flicking → Leads to wide, inefficient loops. Keep your wrist firm.
Not Pausing on the Back Cast → The line won't fully extend, creating weak casts.
Overpowering the Cast → A smooth, controlled motion beats brute strength every time.

Dropping the Rod Tip Too Early → Leads to a low, ineffective cast. Keep the rod up until the loop unrolls.

The Roll Cast: No Room? No Problem!

Imagine you're standing in a river, and there's a tree right behind you. What do you do?

You roll cast.

✓ Start with Rod Tip Low – Line should be straight in front of you on the water. The friction of the water and the line will load your rod.

✓ Lift rod hand and rod tip to shoulder height slightly behind you – You rod should be slightly offset. This forms the D Loop.

✓ Stop and Pop! – Come to a complete stop before driving the rod forward.

✓ Smoothly Drive the Rod Forward – Stop at 10 o'clock, letting the line unroll.

✓ The tighter your D loop, the more power your roll cast will have.

✓ The larger your D loop the more slack you will have in your line.

Common Mistakes

- Not offsetting rod tip causing the fly to hit you in the back or the back of the head.
- Not pausing for a brief second or two.
- Driving the rod tip into the ground or into the water. You are better off finishing off the cast with your rod tip at 10 O'clock.

False Casting, Shooting Line & Line Control

Now it's time to bring it all together. If you've mastered the overhead cast and the roll cast, you're already well on your way. Nail down this final section, and you'll be on the verge of becoming a true fly casting pro.

False casting is making a series of overhead casts, forward and back casts without letting the line hit the ground or water. This will teach you line control, stripping, mending and feeding line. Once again, if you are visual learner search fly casting on the internet and watch You Tube Videos.

False Cast: Keeps the fly dry and lets you adjust distance and direction.

Shooting Line: Smoothly release extra line for longer casts.

Line control: Teaches you how to use your rod hand and line hand together as a team.

A Beginner's Drill for Mastering False Casting, Shooting Line and Line Control

1. Start Short: Begin with only 15 feet of line out of the rod tips. Pull another 15 feet of rod out from your reel.
2. Start an overhead cast without letting line hit the ground on forward of back cast. When your timing is right on false casting open and close your line hand on the forward cast, so your cast does not collapse. Line should be let out in increments.
3. Watch Your Loops: Keep your line tight and loops narrow.
4. End with a Target: Land the fly on a specific spot, practicing precision. Remember, your rod follows your tip.
5. Once your line hits the water, you'll have about 20 feet of line out. Take your line hand, put the line through it, and start stripping it in with short, controlled increments until you have about 10 feet of line out.
6. From there, you can pick up the line and start another false cast, repeating the process. This drill helps you develop line control and teaches you how to shoot line for extra distance—a key skill for improving your fly casting

Congratulations! You've done it! Now that you've mastered the overhead cast, roll cast, and false casting, you've reached a new level in your fly fishing journey. These are the core skills that separate a beginner from a true fly fisher. With these techniques under your belt, you're no longer just casting—you're fishing with purpose, precision, and confidence. Well done!

Fly Fishing can be passed on as family tradition

9
Presentation and Specialty Casts

Loop Control: The Secret to Distance and Presentation

The loop is your signature—it tells everything about your skill. A loop in fly casting is the shape your fly line makes in the air as it unrolls during the cast. Think of it like a traveling J shape—the top leg is the leading edge, and the bottom leg follows underneath.

Why Loops Matter

- Loops dictate everything—how your fly lands, how well it cuts through wind, and how naturally it drifts.
- Tight loops – Precision, wind penetration, and added distance.
- Open loops – Soft landings for delicate presentations, poor wind penetration, and limited distance.

Tailing Loop: Caused by Poor Timing

A tailing loop usually happens due to poor timing in the cast—either too quick or too slow. If you rush the forward cast before the rod fully loads on the back cast, the loop collapses and crosses over itself. On the other hand, if you delay too long, the rod loses energy, causing the loop to drop and tangle.

How to Fix It:

✅ Smooth and steady timing – Let the rod fully load on the back cast before starting the forward cast. The line should uncoil completely behind you before you begin forward.

✅ **Feel the rod load** – Wait until you feel the rod flex and store energy before beginning the forward stroke.

✅ **Gradual power application** – Start the forward cast slowly, then increase speed smoothly rather than using a sudden burst of power.

The Haul: More Speed, More Distance, Less Effort!

What is a Haul? A haul is a quick downward pull on the fly line with your non-casting hand. The double haul means you do it twice:

First Haul → During the back cast.

The haul is a great way for beginners to quickly increase line speed and improve casting distance. Start with a single haul on the forward cast:

1. As you make your forward cast, use your line hand to give a quick, firm pull on the line as the rod loads.
2. This boosts line speed and helps shoot more line with less effort.
3. Release the line at the right moment to maximize distance and maintain a tight loop.

Pro Tip: Once you've mastered the single haul, you're ready to take it to the next level with the double haul. This advanced technique will give you even greater control, distance, and finesse in your casting. At this point, you've become the conductor of the orchestra—every movement of your rod and line working in harmony, creating a seamless and powerful cast.

Second Haul → During the forward cast.

This adds speed and power, helping you punch through the wind.

Step-by-Step: Mastering the Double Haul

The Back Cast Haul

✓ Lift the rod smoothly.
✓ Accelerate back to 1 o'clock.
✓ Quick tug on the line as the rod moves back.
✓ Release the line so it shoots freely.

The Forward Cast Haul

✓ Let the line fully straighten behind you (pause!).
✓ Start the forward cast smoothly.
✓ Haul down again as the rod moves forward.
✓ Let go and let the line shoot forward!

Mending: Mastering the Drift

Mending keeps your fly drifting naturally by repositioning your line on the water. It's the most important aspect of fly fishing. A perfect cast means nothing if your fly doesn't drift naturally. That's where mending comes in.

Upstream Mend – Slows down a drag-heavy drift.

Downstream Mend – Speeds up the fly to match the current.

Stack Mend – Adds slack for a long, drag-free drift.

Loop Control & Drift

Most of you think it's about distance, but it's not. It's about precision. If your fly lands with a splash, you will spook the trout. If it drags across the surface, they won't even consider it. But if you get it right—if that fly drifts perfectly—you'll have a real chance of fooling a trout.

Pro Tip: Mend in the Air for a Better Drift

If you throw your line out like a rope, you'll have less than a second before your fly starts to drag. Beginners usually mend on the water after the line lands, but this often costs valuable time and can disturb the water.

As you progress to an intermediate level, you'll learn to mend in the air before your line or fly touches down. This involves:

1. After your forward cast, use a quick flick of the rod tip to reposition the line mid-air.
2. This creates slack or adjusts the line's position, setting up a natural drift before the line even hits the water.
3. Air mending reduces drag, improves presentation, and increases your chances of a strike.

Mastering the air mend separates casual anglers from seasoned fly fishers—it's a game-changer for achieving a perfect drift.

Upstream Mend: Fix Drag Before It Starts

Purpose: Prevents the current from pulling your fly unnaturally.

How to Upstream Mend:

- Cast across or slightly upstream.
- Lift your rod tip to pick up slack.
- Flip the line upstream with a quick wrist motion.
- Repeat if needed during the drift.

Downstream Mend: Keep It Natural

Purpose: Lets your fly drift naturally in slower currents while your line is in faster water.

How to Downstream Mend:

- Cast slightly upstream or across the current.
- Watch how the current moves your line.
- Use a quick wrist flick to push the line downstream.
- Adjust mends as needed for a longer drift.
- Good when you want your fly to drag on purpose.

Stack Mending: Extending the Drift

Stack mending is the technique of performing multiple mends during a single drift to extend the natural presentation of your fly. Instead of making one large mend, you add small, repeated mends to feed slack into the line and keep the fly drifting naturally.

Reach Mend Cast: Set Up a Better Drift From the Start

The purpose of the reach mend cast is to adjust your line position before it even touches the water to create a natural, drag-free drift. To mend, wait until the end of your forward cast, then extend your rod tip upstream or downstream depending on the current direction. This subtle movement places slack exactly where you need it, helping your fly drift naturally with the current and increasing your chances of a strike.

Puddle Cast: More Drift, Less Drag

A well-executed puddle cast works because it reduces drag, keeping your drift natural, ensures a soft landing that won't spook fish, and extends the drift by keeping your fly in the strike zone longer. To do it right, cast high, aiming just above your target. Stop high to create slack, then drop your rod tip quickly to allow the line to puddle softly on the water. This technique is especially effective for upstream drifts, mixed currents, and clear, shallow water where presentation matters most. A higher stop creates more slack, giving you better control over the drift. Combine this with well-timed mends to keep your fly drifting naturally and increase your chances of a take.

Wiggle Cast: Adding Slack for the Perfect Drift

Some currents are just plain tricky—faster in some places, slower in others. If your fly moves unnaturally, a trout will see that. That's where the wiggle cast comes in.

Using this technique reduces drag, keeping your fly drifting naturally, which helps fool wary fish by creating a lifelike presentation. It also extends the drift by adding slack, giving your fly more time in the strike zone. To execute it, cast normally, aiming slightly above your target. Then, add wiggles by shaking the rod tip side to side—use slow, wide wiggles for gentle currents and tight, fast wiggles for faster water. Let the line settle into natural S-curves on the water and adjust as needed with a mend to control drag and maintain a smooth drift.

Mastering specialty casts means learning to execute them from both the forward and backhand side, which becomes especially important in windy conditions. If the wind is blowing from your casting side, a forward cast can cause the line to blow into you—making a backhand cast the better option. Conversely, if the wind is coming from the opposite side, a forward cast will help keep the line away from your body. Being able to switch between forward and backhand casts depending on wind direction gives you better control, improves accuracy, and helps you avoid tangles (or getting hooked). To be effective, you need to be accurate with both casts—and that starts with understanding the line follows the rod tip. Wherever your rod tip finishes, that's where your line will go. Learning to control the rod tip with precision is key to consistent, accurate casting in any condition.

Using specialty casts, you can achieve better drifts and catch more fish.

10
Fly Fishing Apparel & Accessories

Gearing Up: The Right Tools & Apparel for Success

Now that you've mastered rod, reel, line selection, knots, terminal tackle, fly rod rigging, and casting, it's time to dial in your accessories and apparel. Having the right setup keeps you comfortable, prepared, and focused on catching fish—not battling the elements. In this next section, you'll learn about:

Essential Accessories – Tools like nippers, forceps, tippet holders, and fly boxes.

Waders & Boots – Staying dry and stable in the water.

Apparel for All Conditions – Layering, sun protection, and weatherproof gear.

Jackets & Vests – Carrying your gear efficiently.

Fly Fishing Apparel: Dressing for Success

Layer up like a pro—just like building the perfect pizza pie!

Dressing in layers keeps you comfortable, protected, and ready for any conditions. And what better way to understand layering than by comparing it to a mouth-watering, fully loaded pizza?

The Crust – The Base Layer: Just like a good pizza starts with a solid crust, your base layer is the foundation of your fishing comfort. It wicks moisture, regulates temperature, and keeps you dry. Think synthetic fabrics—no cotton allowed!

The Sauce – The Insulating Layer: The sauce brings the flavor—and in this case, brings the warmth. Whether it's a fleece, down, or synthetic mid-layer, this piece traps heat while staying breathable, ensuring you stay warm without overheating.

The Cheese – The Outer Layer: The cheese holds everything together, just like a good waterproof shell. Your outer layer shields you from wind, rain, and sun, keeping you fishing longer no matter the weather. Breathable, windproof, and water-resistant are the keys here.

The Toppings – The Accessories: What's a pizza without toppings? Accessories make the experience complete. This includes:

Headwear – Sun hats, beanies, or buffs for protection.

Fingerless Gloves – Keep your hands warm but maintain dexterity.

Sun Apparel – UPF-rated shirts, neck gaiters, and arm sleeves.

Socks – Wool socks keep feet warm in cold water.

The Final Drizzle – Specialty Gear: Just like that extra drizzle of olive oil or balsamic glaze, these essentials bring everything together:

Waders – Stay dry while wading.

Wading Boots – Provide grip and stability.

Wading Belt – Safety first—prevents water from rushing in if you take a spill.

Vest or Pack – Keeps your gear organized and accessible.

The Parmesan Sprinkle – The Tools: Every great pizza needs a final touch of Parmesan cheese, red pepper or oregano, just like every angler needs their essential tools:

Nippers & Zingers – Cut tippet and keep tools handy.

Forceps – Remove hooks safely.

Fly Boxes – Keep your bugs organized and ready to go.

Nets – To properly land your fish.

Just like a perfectly crafted pizza, every layer and accessory has a purpose. Master your layering system along with the right accessories, and you'll be comfortable, prepared, and ready to fish in any condition. Now, let's dig in!

The Evolution of Fly-Fishing Apparel: Staying Warm & Dry

Gone are the days of sweaty cotton base layers and stuffy neoprene waders. Early anglers stayed warm for a time, but at a cost—moisture buildup left them damp and chilled and led to getting cold at 17 times a faster rate.

Today's advancements keep anglers dry, warm, and comfortable with:

Moisture-Wicking Base Layers – Wool or synthetics pull sweat away from the skin.

Breathable Waders – Allow moisture to escape while keeping water out.

Layering Systems – Lightweight, quick-drying layers prevent overheating.

Modern gear means better comfort, longer fishing days, and no more soggy misery!

The Crust: A Solid Base – Essential for Any Style

Just like a base layer, you cannot have a great pizza without a superb crust—whether it's thin, thick, or deep dish—your fly-fishing wardrobe starts with the base layer. This essential piece manages moisture, regulates temperature, and keeps you comfortable on the water.

Base Layers for Every Season

Warm Weather: Lightweight, breathable, UPF-rated for sun protection.

Cold Weather: Midweight or heavyweight thermal layers trap heat while wicking sweat.

Pro Tips for Base Layer Success: Fit Matters – Snug but not restrictive for max moisture wicking and mobility.

A good base layer = all-day comfort = stay dry = stay warm = staying fishing!

The Sauce: Insulating Layers – The Warmth That Brings It All Together

A pizza without a robust, flavor-packed tomato sauce? Unthinkable. Just like fly fishing without a good insulating layer in cooler weather. Your insulating layer is the rich, flavorful sauce that locks in warmth, keeping you comfortable while allowing moisture to escape.

The Key Ingredients – Choosing the Right Insulation

Fleece (Polyester) – Lightweight, breathable, and quick-drying—perfect for moderate cold or active fishing days.

Modern day hoodie, lightweight with SPF sun protection.

Synthetic Insulation (Primaloft, Polartec, etc.) – Stays warm even when damp, making it ideal for variable weather.

How Insulation Works – Trapping Heat, Releasing Moisture

Your body generates heat when moving—your insulating layer traps it in while letting sweat escape, keeping you from getting clammy and cold.

Pro Tips for Maximum Warmth & Comfort

Layer Smart – Pair fleece mid-layers with puffy jackets in extreme cold.

Stay Dry – Insulation works best when dry—use a breathable shell in wet conditions.

Test Your Setup – Try different layer combos in local conditions to see what works best for you.

Like a good sauce on a pizza, your insulating layer brings everything together—keeping you warm, dry, and ready to fish all day.

The Cheese: Outer Shell Layer – The Essential Ingredient

Just as a pizza needs a superb crust for structure and a robust sauce for warmth and depth, it also needs high-quality, delicious cheese to bring it all together. In fly fishing, your outer shell—the rain jacket—is that essential final layer. It protects you from the elements, keeping you dry, warm, and comfortable so you can stay on the water longer.

Why a Quality Shell Matters

A good rain jacket isn't just about staying dry—it's your defense against wind, rain, cold and snow, ensuring your base and insulating layers do their job. Cheap jackets trap sweat and leak in heavy rain. A high-quality shell is a must-have.

What to Look for in an Outer Shell

Waterproof & Breathable – Gore-Tex and similar membranes block rain but let sweat escape, keeping you dry inside and out.

Wind Resistance – Cuts the chill, especially when wading deep or fishing in cold weather.

Stealthy Colors – Earth tones like light green or tan blend with the environment, keeping you concealed from fish.

Pro Tip: Invest in Quality

A $200+ rain jacket might seem steep, but it's worth every penny. When the storm hits, you'll be dry, warm, and still fishing, while others are packing up.

Like cheese on a pizza, a great shell seals the deal, making your fly-fishing apparel system complete, functional, and ready for anything.

The Toppings: Fly Fishing Accessories That Make the Difference

Toppings bring personality and flavor to a pizza, just like fly-fishing accessories complete your gear. While your base, insulating, and outer layers keep you comfortable, accessories protect you from sun, cold, wind, and water. The right extras ensure longer, more comfortable days on the water—without distractions like sunburn, frozen fingers, or soggy feet.

Headwear: Protect yourself from yourself

Warm-Weather Hats – A wide-brimmed straw hat or UPF-rated cap keeps the sun off your face, ears, and neck.

Cold-Weather Hats – A beanie or insulated cap traps heat, keeping you warm on frigid mornings. Layer over a baseball cap for extra versatility.

Fingerless Gloves: Stay Warm, Keep Dexterity

- Cold Days? Fingerless gloves keep hands warm without sacrificing grip and knot-tying ability.
- Sun Protection? Lightweight sun gloves shield against UV rays while keeping hands cool.

Sun Protection: Stay Cool & Covered

Sun Hoodies – UPF-rated, moisture-wicking, and lightweight, a must-have for hot days on the water.

Neck Gaiters (Buffs) – Protect against sun, wind, cold, and even bugs.

Polarized Sunglasses – Essential for reducing glare, spotting fish beneath the surface and protecting from errant flies.

Don't skimp here, you need to spend the money on high quality eyewear.

Socks: Keep Your Feet Happy

Warm-Weather Socks –Synthetic blends wick moisture and prevent blisters.

Cold-Weather Socks – Thicker wool socks insulate while keeping feet dry.

Pro Tip: Avoid cotton—it traps moisture and leads to cold, uncomfortable feet. Always carry an extra pair of socks if you do get your feet wet. On a very cold day wear a thinner pair of socks with a heavier pair and keep your toes moving to stay warm.

Just like the perfect pizza needs toppings, your fly-fishing setup isn't complete without the right accessories. Stay cool in the heat, warm in the cold, and comfortable all day by gearing up with purpose-driven extras that keep you fishing longer and better!

The Final Drizzle: Specialty Gear That Elevates Your Game

Just like a drizzle of olive oil or balsamic takes a pizza from good to gourmet, the right specialty gear transforms your fly-fishing experience from ordinary to exceptional. Specialty gear isn't just about convenience—it enhances safety, efficiency, and endurance, letting you fish longer and more effectively.

Waders: Stay Dry, Stay Fishing

A great pair of breathable Gore-Tex waders is a game-changer, keeping you warm, dry, and comfortable no matter the conditions. Whether wading deep pools or crossing freestone rivers, the right waders unlock better positioning, longer drifts, and improved stealth.

Why Waders Matter:

- Gets you off the bank.
- Reach More Water – Access prime spots other anglers can't.
- Stealth Approach – Move quietly without spooking fish.
- Better Casting Angles – Position yourself for precise presentations.
- Stay Warm & Comfortable – Dry gear = longer fishing sessions

Wading Belt: Small Gear, Big Safety

Think of a wading belt as your seatbelt for the river. It prevents water from filling your waders in case of a fall and even holds tools for quick access. A simple yet essential piece of gear!

Pro Tip: If you say to someone that it's been a long time since you've fallen in, or that you haven't fallen in for years, you probably will be the next to take a dunk!

Wader Bag

Why Gore-Tex® Waders?

Unlike rubber or neoprene, Gore-Tex® waders breathe, keeping you dry inside and out. Higher end models offer durability and reinforced panels, articulated fit and mobility, adjustable shoulder straps and waist belts

Breathable Fabric – Sweat escapes, water stays out.

Durable & Reinforced – Built for rough terrain and long days.

Integrated Gravel Guards – Keep sand and debris out of boots.

Pro Tip: Always air dry your waders after each trip to prevent mildew and extend their lifespan!

A solid set of waders, a wading belt, and breathable materials don't just keep you dry and comfortable—they increase safety, endurance, and access to the best fishing water. With the right specialty gear, you're not just fishing—you're mastering the river.

Wading Boots: Grip, Stability & Comfort

Your boots are your connection to the riverbed—choose wisely! The right pair keeps you upright, stable, and safe as you navigate slippery rocks, swift currents, and uneven terrain.

Sole Options: Pick Your Traction

Felt Soles – Superior grip on slick, algae-covered rocks. (Banned in some areas due to invasive species.)

Rubber Soles – Durable, versatile, and great for winter since snow won't stick.

Studded Soles – Maximum traction for fast-moving, rocky rivers. Available in removable or built-in options.

Key Features to Look For:

Ankle Support – Crucial for rocky terrain.

Drainage Ports – Let water escape, keeping boots light.

Toe & Heel Reinforcement – Shields against impacts.

Pro Tip: Always rinse your boots after fishing different waters to prevent the spread of invasive species.

Fishing Vest or Pack: Organize Your Gear Like a Pro

Are Fishing Vests on Their Way Out?

Once a fly-fishing staple, vests are being replaced by lighter, more mobile options like sling packs and chest packs. While vests still provide tons of storage, many anglers find them bulky and restrictive on long fishing days.

Vest vs. Pack: Which One Fits Your Style?

Boat bag – A great way to organize your gear and keep it dry, whether fishing from shore or a boat.

Fishing Vest – Classic, full-pocket design for easy access.

Sling Pack – Worn across the body, swings forward for quick gear access.

Chest Pack – Compact and minimalist for a clutter-free experience.

Backpack – Best for all-day trips or backcountry adventures.

Key Features to Look For:

Ample Pockets – Stay organized with zippered compartments.

Tool Attachments – D rings & loops for zingers, nippers, and hemostats.

Water-Resistant Material – Essential for protecting phones & cameras.

Wader Bags: Keeping Your Gear Organized & Dry

After a long day on the water, the last thing you want is to throw wet, muddy waders into your car or backpack. A good wader bag helps keep everything organized, contained, and clean.

What a Wader Bag Should Include:

Ventilated Storage: Allows your waders and boots to dry properly without mildew buildup.

Wet & Dry Compartments: Keeps wet gear separate from dry clothing and essentials.

Store you extra gear. Great for carrying and extra towel and change of clothes in case you or your buddy takes a dunk.

Pockets for Extras: Handy storage for socks, wading belts, or extra laces.

Pro Tip: Look for a bag with waterproof lining and reinforced zippers to keep everything secure and protected.

Modern-Day Boat Bags: Keeping Gear Protected & Accessible

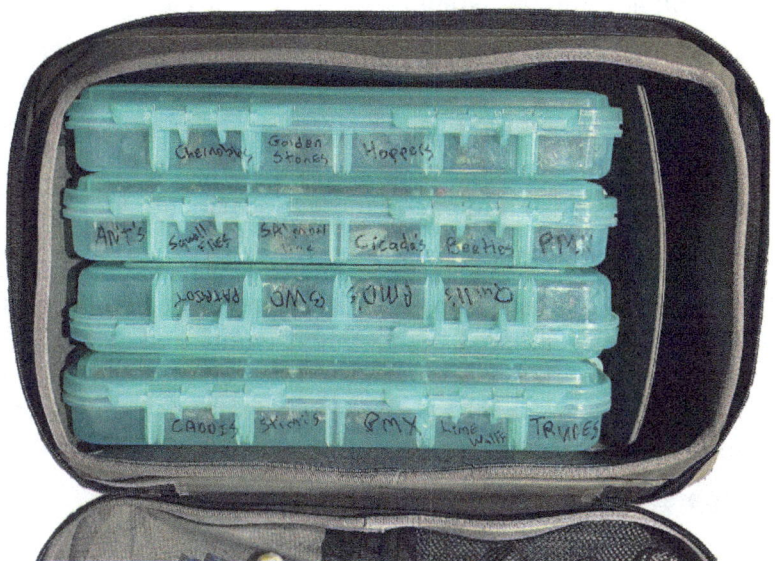

When you're out on the water, whether in a drift boat, raft, or even wading, you need a bag that can handle everything—rain, splashes, and even the occasional dunk. A well-designed boat bag keeps your gear dry, organized, and easily accessible, making your day on the water more efficient and enjoyable.

What to Look for in a Boat Bag:

Waterproof Construction: High-quality boat bags feature welded seams and waterproof zippers to keep gear dry even in rough conditions.

Multiple Compartments: Allows easy organization of fly boxes, extra reels, tools, and essentials.

Non-Slip Base: Prevents sliding around in the boat and adds durability.

External Tool Attachments: Many models have built-in loops and D-rings for quick access to nippers, hemostats, and tippet holders.

Padded Shoulder Strap or Handles: Comfortable to carry when loading and unloading.

You might a beginner, but you will be collecting more gear, so these bags will help keep you organized, regardless of whether you ever own or row a boat.

Pro Tip: Pack your gear the same way every time—so you can find things instantly and spend more time fishing.

The Final Sprinkle: Essential Tools

Just as freshly grated Parmesan cheese completes a pizza, the right tools—nippers, hemostats, zingers, and fly boxes—bring everything together for a smooth day on the water. These essentials may be small, but they make every cast, every knot, and every fish landed feel effortless.

Nippers: Small Tool, Big Impact

Nippers may seem minor, but they're indispensable for trimming tippet, cutting line, and keeping knots tidy. Look for:

- Corrosion-resistant materials (stainless steel or anodized aluminum).
- Ergonomic design for easy use, even with cold or gloved hands.

- Built-in hook eye cleaner for removing excess glue from fly eyes.

Pro Tip: Attach nippers to a zinger on your vest or pack for quick, one-handed access.

Hemostats (Forceps): Essential for Catch-and-Release

Hemostats allow for gentle hook removal, pinching barbs, and handling fish with minimal harm. They're also great for adjusting split shot and other small tasks. Best options:

- Straight, unserrated jaws for precise, safe hook removal.
- Rust-resistant coating for durability in all conditions.
- Locking mechanism to keep them securely closed when not in use.

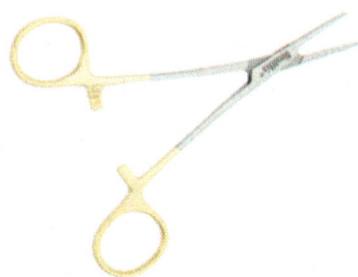

Pro Tip: Keep hemostats handy to remove hooks quickly and minimize fish handling time.

Zingers: Keep Tools Accessible

Zingers act like retractable leashes, ensuring tools like nippers and hemostats stay within reach. No more digging through pockets or losing gear in the river!

Choosing the Right Zinger:

- Stainless steel wire models are far more durable than rope versions.
- Pin-on zingers attach securely to vests, while clip-on models work great for packs and waders.

A good zinger keeps your tools exactly where you need them, so you can focus on fishing, not fumbling.

Fly Boxes: The Heart of Your Arsenal

Your fly box is like a well-stocked spice rack—keeping the right flies organized and ready for action. A good fly box protects your patterns and saves you time on the water.

Types of Fly Boxes:

Foam/Gel Boxes: Lightweight, ideal for securing nymphs.

Magnetic Boxes: Perfect for tiny midges and small flies.

Compartment Boxes: Great for larger dry flies, and streamers.

Waterproof Boxes: Must-have for rainy days and splash-prone conditions. Best for dry flies and nymphs.

Building Your Fly Collection Over Time

When you first start fly fishing, it's tempting to buy every fly in the shop. But the truth is, you don't need to stockpile flies all at once. One well-organized box is enough to start. As you fish more, learn what works, and explore different waters, you'll naturally build your collection over time.

Tips for Expanding Your Fly Collection:

Start Small: A single fly box with essential patterns is enough when you're beginning.

Match the Hatch: Gradually add flies that match the insects in your local waters.

Seasonal Growth: Different flies work in different seasons—expand your selection as you learn.

Stay Organized: Use multiple fly boxes for dry flies, nymphs, and streamers as your collection grows.

Pro Tip: Build Your Fly Collection with Expert Help

Visit your local fly shop and let the shop dog (or the local expert) know where and when you're fishing. They can help you select a dozen flies in four different patterns and sizes tailored to the season and local hatch. If you do this several times throughout the year, you'll gradually build up a well-rounded collection of flies that will cover a variety of conditions and hatches—setting you up for success no matter when or where you fish. Plus, supporting your local fly shop keeps the community strong and connected.

Clear Gel Coat Fly Boxes: Simple & Functional

As your fly collection grows, organization is key. Clear gel coat fly boxes make fly selection easy while keeping your patterns secure and dry.

Why They're Awesome:

- Great for nymphs.
- Transparent lid allows for quick fly selection without opening the box.
- Gel coat interior holds flies in place, preventing damage.
- Waterproof sealing keeps delicate flies protected in wet conditions.

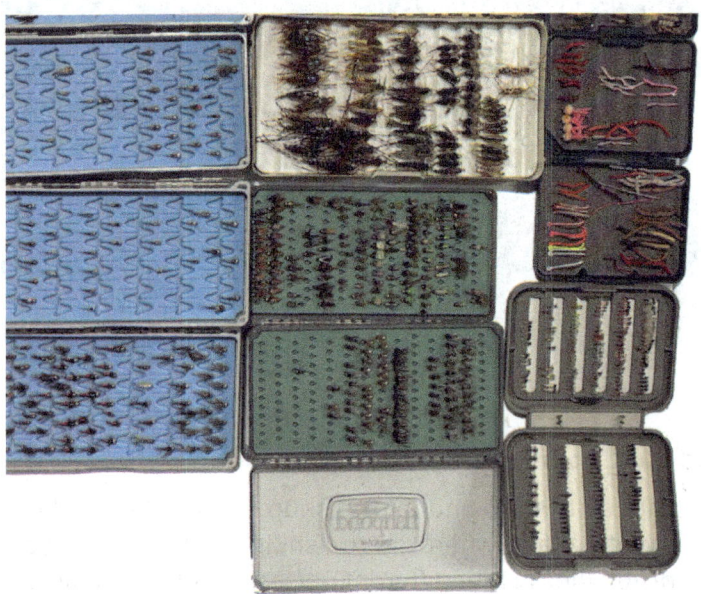

A well-organized fly box means less time searching and more time fishing. Whether you're fine-tuning your selection or building a go-to system, these boxes make life on the water easier. Once you have grown out of one box, you can organize your fly types into multiple boxes.

Wading Staffs: Stay Balanced, Stay Fishing

A wading staff is your third leg in the river, giving you extra stability on slippery rocks and strong currents. Whether you're crossing a fast-moving stream or wading deep into unknown waters, a sturdy staff prevents slips and keeps you upright.

Collapsible & Lightweight: Easy to store, ready when needed.

Durable Materials: Aluminum or carbon fiber for long-lasting strength.

Confidence Booster: Move safely in the river or on the bank so you can focus on fishing, not your footing.

Hiking Staff: Doubles as a hiking staff to get to and from the river.

Pro tips: Attach your wading staff to a retractable lanyard for quick deployment. If you do not have a wading staff, you can grab a stick from the bank to use either when wading or crossing a river.

Tippet Spool Organizer: Tangle-Free & Ready to Go

- No more digging for tippet mid-fish! A spool organizer keeps multiple sizes neatly stored and easily accessible.
- Compact & Clip-On: Attaches to vests, packs, or waders.
- Prevents Tangles: Keeps spools organized and within reach.
- Quick Changes: Swap tippet sizes fast to match changing conditions.

Pro Tip: Look for models with built-in tension bands to keep spools from unraveling.

Polarized Sunglasses: See More, Catch More

Glare is your worst enemy on the water. Polarized sunglasses cut through reflections, letting you see fish, structure, and riverbeds with total clarity.

Safety First: Protects your eyes from UV rays, wind, and errant hooks.

Fish Spotting Power: See beneath the surface like never before.

Better Wading: Improved depth perception means safer steps in tricky currents.

Use a *Handy Map Microfiber Cloth* to keep your glasses clean and dry. **Visit www.mapthexperience.com**

Pro Tip: Use a lanyard to keep your shades secure and within reach at all times.

Magnetic Glasses: No More Squinting at Tiny Flies

Struggling to thread that tippet through a size 22 hook eye? Magnetic glasses flip down or click together for instant magnification, making fly tying quick and painless.

Hands-Free Zoom: Flip down when needed, flip up when you're done.

Click designs: Snap together.

No More Eye Strain: Perfect for low-light conditions and tiny flies.

Convenient & Fast: Attaches magnetically for instant clarity.

Pro Tip: Keep a pair of click one on a lanyard hanging on your neck.

Choosing the Right Net: Handle Fish with Care

A good net isn't just about landing fish—it's about protecting them for a safe release. Rubber mesh nets are the gold standard for ethical fly fishing, offering a gentle, tangle-free solution that's easy on both fish and gear.

Why Rubber Nets Are the Best

Fish-Friendly: Unlike nylon, rubber mesh won't remove slime coatings or damage scales.

Tangle-Free: No more snagged flies or tangled hooks.

Quick & Safe Handling: Makes catch-and-release faster and less stressful for the fish.

Lightweight: Made of lightweight, extremely durable material.

Picking the Right Net for Your Fishing Style

Float Fishermen: A long-handle rubber net provides extra reach for landing fish from a drift boat or raft.

Wading Anglers: A short-handle net with a magnetic net release keeps it secure and easy to grab.

Rainbow Trout in a Rubber Net

11
Reading a Trout Stream

Trout don't just swim aimlessly through the river, hoping to bump into a meal. Their entire existence revolves around three things: oxygen, safety and food. If you understand how they get those three things, you'll know exactly where to find them.

Oxygen: The Lifeline of a Trout

Unlike humans, trout don't have the luxury of pulling air straight from the sky. They extract oxygen from the water as it moves over their gills, which means they need clean, cold, well-oxygenated water. The best places to find them are in riffles, fast-moving runs, and deeper pools where fresh, aerated water keeps them comfortable.

When the water gets too warm or stagnant, trout begin to struggle. They become lethargic, stressed, and far less likely to feed. In extreme cases, they retreat to the deepest, coolest parts of the river—or they die.

Predators: Constantly on Guard

Trout don't just worry about oxygen—they spend every moment of their lives on high alert. They're not just avoiding fly fishers with fly rods; they're dodging a whole lineup of predators:

Otters & Mink – Stealthy hunters that prowl the water.

Eagles, Hawks and Ospreys – Precision killers from above, ready to snatch an exposed fish in seconds.

A Trout's Guide to the River: The Best Real Estate

Trout don't waste energy sitting in bad water. They position themselves in spots where food drifts to them, where they don't have to fight the current, and where they can disappear in an instant.

Trout will change position in the water column depending on the hatch, starting lower in the water column early in the day and gradually moving up as the hatch progresses. As insects become more active and begin emerging, trout rise to intercept them, eventually feeding right at the surface when the hatch is in full swing.

That old saying, *"90% of the fish are in 10% of the water,"* is absolutely true. Here's where to look:

Seams – The Food Highway

Think of a boulder in the stream, where two seams are created—these are the food highways of the river. Where fast and slow currents meet, insects naturally drift downstream, concentrating in these seams. Trout position themselves in the slower water just outside the main current, conserving energy while effortlessly picking off passing bugs. Understanding these feeding lanes is key to presenting your fly where trout are actively feeding.

Pillows – Also known as fulcrum

A pillow, also called a fulcrum, is the cushion of slower water that forms directly in front of a rock or other obstruction. As the current splits around the obstacle, the water in front of it slows down, creating a small pocket where trout can hold with minimal effort.

Eddies – The All-You-Can-Eat Buffet

An eddy forms where the current wraps around and flows back upstream against the main flow. These swirling pockets of slower water—often found along river bends—create natural collection points for drifting insects, much like a conveyor belt. Trout take advantage of these calm zones, holding in place and feeding with minimal effort. Eddies can be especially productive in the spring when high water pushes fish out of the stronger currents and into these sheltered feeding areas.

Undercut Banks – The Hidden Café

Shade, safety, and food all in one. These banks provide trout with a sheltering lie from predators while offering a good supply of drifting insects.

Riffles – The Natural Camouflage

Fast-moving, choppy water provides a continuous flow of food, carrying insects downstream in a steady supply. Riffles, in particular, are where hatches begin, as insects emerge from the riverbed and rise toward the surface. The broken water also acts as natural camouflage, hiding trout from predators and anglers alike. Once a hatch starts, trout will follow the drifting bugs, often moving downstream into slower water where they can feed more efficiently. Understanding this progression helps fly fishers anticipate where trout will be actively feeding as the hatch develops.

Drop-Offs – Sudden depth changes where shallow water drops into a deeper pool. Trout use these as ambush points, sitting just below the drop to intercept food drifting from above.

Deep Pools – The Cozy Hideaway

When trout need to rest, they drop into deep pools at the tail end of a run. These areas provide safety, concealment, and easy access to drifting food.

Runs & Glides – Runs are steady, medium-speed currents that provide ideal feeding lanes. Glides are slower, smoother sections just downstream of runs where trout can feed more cautiously.

Tail outs – The shallow, tapering end of a pool before the next riffle.

Show Time – Approaching the River

By now, you're dressed like a fly fisher, *at least your spouse thinks you are*. You have your rod, reel, rigging dialed in, you've mastered your knots, and you've got the right accessories—

polarized sunglasses to cut glare and spot fish, a vest or pack stocked with essentials, and the right layers to keep you comfortable. But before you even think about stepping into the river, stop and observe—this is just as important as making a perfect cast. Too many fly fishers rush in, disturbing fish and ruining their chances before they even make a presentation.

Do you see any insects on the way to the stream, in the air or on the water? Are fish rising? A subtle sip on the surface could mean trout are feeding on midges or mayflies, while splashier rises might indicate caddis activity. If you notice fish flashing just below the surface, they could be targeting emergers or pupae. Look closely—do you see bugs floating on the surface? Are fish heads breaking through the water?

That shop dog at the fly shop you just visited recommended a fly that might have been good yesterday, but it doesn't mean it's the right fly for this time and day. *Be patient*. The weather, light, or time of day might not be ideal for the fly you tied on. Trout can be picky, and their feeding patterns change. If your first choice isn't working, observe the water again, and don't be afraid to adjust.

Pro tip: Wait until you get to the river to tie on your dropper fly, once you decide what is hatching, if anything.

Also, take a moment to look for signs of recent activity. Fresh footprints on the bank or disturbed water could mean another fly fisher has already fished this spot, making the trout more cautious. Scan the river—do you see another fly fisherman upstream or downstream? If so, they may have already worked your water and moved on, especially if they are upstream of you. Now, you might want to move to a less pressured area.

Every day we fish, we learn. Becoming a master will take time.

Having the right gear is essential but knowing how to read the water and observe your surroundings is what separates a good fly fisher from a great one. Take your time, be patient, and study the river before making your first move. The more you observe, the better your chances of matching the hatch, presenting the right fly, and fooling a wary trout.

Stepping into the River

Now that we've determined the right fly to match the hatch, it's time to step into the river—but do so quietly. Move carefully between rocks, stepping softly to avoid sending shockwaves through the water. Trout are highly sensitive to movement and vibration, so ease in without creating unnecessary disturbance.

Once you're in position, work the water incrementally—start close and gradually cast farther, covering the river methodically. There's no need to cast a mile; instead, use your waders and boots to adjust your position so you can make accurate, efficient casts.

If you're dry fly fishing, make sure your fly is properly treated with floatant gel and riding high on the water. Keep your line, rod, and shadow away from the fish to avoid spooking them, and limit excessive false casts. Precision and delicacy matter more than distance.

If you're nymphing, ensure your rig is set up correctly—your weight is adjusted properly, and your indicator depth is dialed in so your flies drift naturally without snagging. Work the water patiently; sometimes, it takes multiple drifts before a trout commits to your fly. Avoid lining the fish, which means casting directly over the top of them—instead, use the reach cast, mending techniques, and subtle adjustments you've already learned to achieve a natural drift.

Above all, keep your profile low whenever possible. Trout are always on alert, and the biggest fish typically hold in the best lies—prime feeding zones where they can push smaller trout aside. These dominant fish won't tolerate competition, which is why trophy trout are often found in the most strategic and hardest to reach locations within a pool.

By moving carefully, reading the water, and making deliberate, well-placed casts, you'll greatly increase your chances of success on the river.

Reading the River for More Hookups

If you want to catch trout, don't waste time fishing empty water. Learn to read the river. Look for current breaks, seams, structure, and depth changes. The fish aren't randomly scattered; they are exactly where the conditions are best. The more you understand their habits, the better you'll be at putting your fly in front of them.

ROY

12
Dry Fly Fishing

Why Dry Fly Fishing?

Dry fly fishing is any time your fly is floating on the surface.

Watching a trout rise to take a dry fly is one of the most thrilling experiences in fly fishing. Success requires accurate casting, a drag-free drift, a solid understanding of fish behavior, and precise timing. Proper timing is crucial because setting the hook too early can spook the fish, while waiting too long can result in a missed opportunity. Reading the trout's behavior, anticipating its movements, and reacting at the right moment all play a role in mastering this delicate art. When everything aligns—the cast, the drift, and the timing—the result is an unforgettable connection between fly fisher and trout.

Key Elements of Dry Fly Fishing

Match the Hatch: Observe insects on the water and choose a fly that matches size, shape, color and action.

Presentation Matters: A natural drift is crucial—any unnatural movement can lead to refusals.

Stealth & Approach: Move slowly, stay low, and use the correct leader length to avoid spooking fish.

Adapt to Conditions: Adjust your strategy for wind, water levels, and light conditions.

Look for cloudy days as insects will be hatching.

Casting & Presentation

Soft Landings: A gentle presentation prevents spooking fish.

Timing the Cast: Place the fly just upstream of a rising fish. Avoid casting your line (lining) over the fish.

Mending the Line: Prevents drag and ensures a natural drift.

False Cast- Keeps your fly dry, adjusting for distance and shooting the line.

Upstream Mend: Slows the fly in faster currents.

Downstream Mend: Speeds up the fly in slower water.

Reach Cast: Keeps the line out of conflicting currents, helping maintain a drag-free drift.

Wait Before Setting the Hook: A brief pause ensures the fish has fully taken the fly.

Observe the Rise Form: Gentle sips may require a longer pause, while splashy takes need a quicker but gentler set.

Controlled Hook Set: Lift the rod smoothly—no aggressive jerks.

Be aware of the fish wanting to run. If he does lead him with a high rod tip.

Keep Line Tension: Slack allows the fish to escape.

13
Nymph Fishing

Why Nymph Fishing?

Trout feed 90% of the time below the surface, making nymphing one of the most effective underwater fly fishing techniques.

- Works year-round, even when dry fly fishing is slow.
- A more popular way to fly fish.
- Less affected by weather conditions like wind and bright sun.

Key Elements of Nymph Fishing

Match the Hatch: Choose nymphs that mimic natural insect stages (larva, nymph, emerger).

Drag-Free Drift: Nymphs should move naturally with the current—adjust weight, leader length, and mends as needed.

Strike Detection: Use indicators to feel for subtle takes—set the hook at any hesitation.

Adjust for Depth: If fish aren't biting, adjust indicator depth before switching flies.

Target Feeding Zones: Fish hold near structure (rocks, logs, pools) where currents bring food. Fish will move up and down in the current at various levels. Adjust your flies accordingly.

Indicator Nymphing (Best for Beginners)

How It Works: When using a strike indicator to detect subtle strikes, cast upstream and mend your line to ensure a natural drift, carefully watching for even the slightest movement to set the hook. Adjust your indicator placement to roughly 1.5 to 2 times the depth of the water, positioning your fly accurately in the strike zone, which can vary based on what the fish are feeding on. Employ the "shotgun technique" by repeatedly casting to productive spots, as trout often group in prime feeding areas—be patient and persistent, and don't abandon a promising run too soon.

Common Mistakes: Avoid casting too much line, as it creates excessive drag and makes mending more difficult. Using too much weight results in frequent snags, whereas insufficient weight prevents your flies from reaching the strike zone, leading to fewer bites. Similarly, setting your indicator too shallow will keep your fly above the feeding fish, reducing your chances of success. Always mend your line properly to achieve a natural drift and be careful to keep excess line off the water, particularly in areas where you believe fish are holding.

Euro Nymphing (Tight-Line Nymphing)

How It Works: Lead and follow the drift with your rod tip, maintaining a semi-tight line for effective strike detection. Without an indicator, use direct contact techniques with heavy tungsten jig flies to instantly feel strikes. Employ long leaders, typically ranging from 12 to 20 feet, often combined with a brightly colored tippet section rather than a traditional bobber for visual assistance. Keep as much line as possible off the water to achieve the most natural drift and enhance sensitivity to subtle bites.

Common Mistakes: Avoid having too much slack in your leader, as it leads to missed strikes and reduces your sensitivity to subtle bites. Ensure your flies have adequate weight; if they're too light, they won't reach the bottom where fish often feed. Lastly, don't overcomplicate your drift—allow your flies to move naturally with the current for the best chance of success.

High-Sticking

How It Works: Use short casts, typically between 10 to 20 feet, with your rod tip held high to maintain a tight line, ensuring no fly line touches the water. This approach eliminates slack, making it easier to detect strikes and achieve successful hook-ups. By keeping direct control over the drift, this method is particularly effective when fishing small streams or fast-moving water.

Swinging Nymphs

How It Works: Cast slightly upstream and across, allowing your fly to drift naturally downstream. Once your fly reaches the end of its downstream drift and you begin to feel the gentle pull of the current on your line, slowly lift your rod tip—this upward movement imitates emerging insects such as caddisflies or swimming mayflies like BWOs and PMDs. A swinging presentation can often be essential to effectively matching the hatch. Soft hackle flies are particularly effective for this technique, as they're specifically designed for use as swinging nymphs.

Pro Tips for Nymph Fishing Success

Focus on Depth – If you're not hitting the bottom occasionally, you could be fishing too shallow.

Use Two Nymphs (Tandem Rig) – A larger fly (stonefly) paired with a smaller one (mayfly/midge) increases success.

Vary Presentation – Change drift speed, depth, or fly size if fish aren't responding.

Set the Hook Quickly – Unlike dry fly fishing, nymph takes are subtle—set the hook at any hesitation.

Use a Drag-Free Drift – Mend your line often.

When nymphing upstream line tends to collect at your feet at the end of your drift. We suggest picking up your line slowly by lifting the flyrod and be ready because you will get a lot of strikes on the lift.

Mastering nymph fishing means understanding trout behavior, adjusting techniques, and maintaining a natural drift. With practice, it becomes one of the most productive fly fishing methods available, but it is one of the most difficult to master.

14
Streamer Fishing

Why Fish Streamers?

When there are no active hatches or when the water becomes off-color or murky, streamers can be highly effective. These flies mimic natural prey like baitfish, trout fry, leeches, and crayfish, triggering aggressive responses from predatory trout. Cast and retrieve streamers actively, imitating the swimming action of prey with varying retrieves to attract attention. Because they work well in challenging conditions, streamers are often a great choice when targeting larger trout, especially in low visibility conditions or between insect hatches.

Streamer Fishing Techniques

The Swing *(Great for Deep Runs)*

When streamer fishing, we typically cast slightly up and across stream allowing the fly to work down and across toward instream cover or the opposite bank. Using a smooth strip-and-pause technique, we create a lifelike movement that entices strikes. Keep your rod tip close to the water when stripping. Let the fly swing naturally across the current. At the end of the drift lift your rod tip slowly. Many strikes will occur as the fly rises towards the surface.

Pro tip: It's important to note that smaller fish and fry rarely swim upstream to evade predators; instead, they instinctively dart downstream. By mimicking this natural movement with a well-placed streamer, we can effectively trigger predatory instincts in larger fish.

Additionally, varying retrieve speed, incorporating erratic twitches, and adjusting depth based on water conditions can increase success when targeting aggressive feeders.

The Strip Retrieve

Cast slightly across and upstream, allowing your fly to sink to the desired depth. Once at the right depth, retrieve the fly by stripping the line either with short, fast pulls or long, slow ones. Maintain control of your line, feeling for subtle takes, and don't forget that pauses often trigger strikes, especially as the fly moves upward through the water column.

The Dead Drift *(Best for Slower Pools)*

Cast your fly slightly upstream, allowing it to sink to the desired depth. Mend your line as needed to maintain a natural drift. As the streamer swings downstream, let it move naturally with the current, occasionally adding slight twitches to imitate wounded prey. Keep your rod tip low, ready to detect strikes, and use pauses and gentle lifts to mimic natural movement, enticing trout to strike.

Pro Tips: When fishing streamers, use a short, stout leader to maintain control and effectively handle heavier flies—typically a robust leader around 0X to 2X works well. In general, match your fly's color and size to seasonal and water conditions; during spring and early summer, opt for colors that resemble local prey. After summer rains, when water becomes cloudy, streamer fishing can be particularly effective as trout become aggressive and opportunistic in turbid conditions. Colors that are bright or flashy patterns can excel during periods of off-colored water caused by runoff or storms.

Black Wooly Bugger – World's most popular streamer

15
Hooking – Playing – Landing Trout

The Hook Set: The Final Test

Once you've learned to cast, mend, and control your drift, a strike is inevitable. Now comes the critical moment: setting the hook.

Nymph Fishing

Strike Often – If you're fishing nymphs, you should be setting the hook at the slightest indication of a take. Even a subtle pause, twitch, or hesitation of the indicator could mean a fish has taken your fly.

Err on the Side of Action – Many beginner fly fishers miss strikes simply because they hesitate. If in doubt, set the hook!

Set Once Per Cast – Ideally, you should be making at least one hook set at the end of the drift to avoid missing subtle takes.

Dry Fly Fishing

See the Take, Then Set – With dry flies, you'll typically see the fish rise and take the fly. Unlike nymph fishing, where strikes can be subtle, dry fly takes are visual.

Patience is Key: Setting the Hook in Dry Fly Fishing

One of the most common mistakes in dry fly fishing is setting the hook too soon. When you see a fish rise to your fly, your instinct may be to immediately yank the rod up—but this often pulls the fly right out of the fish's mouth.

How to Avoid a Premature Hook Set

Let the Fish Take the Fly – Instead of reacting instantly, give the fish a moment to close its mouth before lifting the rod. A good rule of thumb is to say, "God Save the Queen" (or count to one) before setting the hook.

Watch the Rise – If the fish takes the fly gently, wait just a fraction longer. If it aggressively smashes the fly, you may need to react slightly faster.

A Smooth Lift, Not a Jerk – Set the hook with a controlled lift of the rod rather than a hard snap. A too-aggressive hook set can break the tippet or pull the fly away before the hook finds purchase.

Streamer Fishing

Strip Set, Not Lift – When fishing streamers, the hook set is different from nymph or dry fly fishing. Instead of lifting the rod, use a strip set by pulling the line with your stripping hand while keeping the rod tip low and to the side.

Side Hook Set – A streamer hook set should be more parallel to the water, pulling to the side rather than straight up. This ensures a solid connection without pulling the fly away from the fish too soon.

Pro Tip: Fly fishing isn't a bass tournament—hook sets should be controlled and purposeful. A smooth lift of the rod for dries and nymphs, and a sideways strip set for streamers, will lead to more successful hookups.

The Proper Way to Fight a Trout: Once you've hooked a trout, the battle is on, and your job is to land the fish quickly and efficiently while minimizing stress and exhaustion. The key to a successful fight is maintaining constant tension on the line.

Keep Your Rod High: Hold your rod at a 45-degree angle, which provides the right balance of control and flexibility. This angle helps absorb the fish's runs and keeps pressure on it without over-exerting the rod or leader. Your rod, reel and tippet all have elasticity built into them to fight the trout.

Let the Fish Run, But Stay in Control: If the trout surges, allow it to take line while keeping gentle pressure with your tip. Your reel's drag system, or manual line management if you're fishing without a drag, will help regulate this pressure. Never clamp down too hard or reel against a running fish or you risk breaking the tippet.

If the Fish Comes Toward You, Strip Line: A trout may suddenly change direction and swim toward you. In this case, be ready to strip in line quickly or reel to maintain tension. A slack line can result in a lost fish. If the fish sees you, its natural instinct is to run, so be prepared to let out line. Your inclination may be to keep pulling but remember—this is a fight between you and the fish. Too much pressure can result in a break-off. Instead, avoid tangles and guide the trout where you want it using your rod tip.

Keep the Fish in the Middle of the Water Column: Avoid letting the fish dive toward the riverbed, where it can snag on rocks, logs, or debris. Use your rod to guide the trout, keeping it in open water where you have control. Play the fish in the middle of the water column until it is ready to be netted. Your goal is to have the shortest amount of line out when playing the fish as this will give you the most control.

Avoid Fast Currents: If the fish heads for strong rapids, try to steer it toward calmer water. If necessary, follow the fish downstream to a place where you can manage the fight more effectively.

Lead the Fish, Don't Force It: Use your rod tip to gently guide the trout rather than overpowering it. Leading the fish allows you to dictate its movements without putting excessive strain on your tackle. It is tough to say when the tippet will break. This is a learning curve, because it will happen. You will never know how much pressure it takes to break off a fish until you experience it.

The Jumping Fish – "Bow to the King": If the trout leaps from the water, quickly lower your rod tip to reduce tension on the line. This is often called *"bowing to the fish."* A tight line mid-air can pull the hook free, so let the fish jump, then regain control when it reenters the water.

The Final Moments: As the fish tires, use steady pressure to guide it toward you. Avoid dragging the fish onto dry land—keep it in the water as much as possible. A net helps to secure the catch safely and allows for an easier, low-impact release. Always net the fish head first or it will swim away from you.

By following these techniques, you'll not only improve your chances of landing more fish but also respect the fish and the sport by ensuring a fair fight and a responsible release.

Landing a Trout Successfully

Now that the fish is tired and (hopefully) in calmer water, it's time for the final and most crucial step—landing it. Rushing this moment can undo all your hard work, so patience and precision are key.

Don't Reach Too Early: One of the most common mistakes anglers make is trying to net the fish too soon. A trout with too much energy left can bolt at the last second, potentially breaking off or getting caught in the current. Keep the fish under control, ensuring it's tired enough before making your move.

Control the Fish with Your Rod: Most fly fishermen use their right hand to control the rod (for right-handed casters), keeping the rod high and slightly behind the body to maintain tension. This positioning allows you to lead the fish where you want it without exerting too much force.

Bring the Fish's Head to the Surface: As the trout tires, angle your rod to guide its head upward. A trout that has its head above water is far less likely to make a sudden dive. However, avoid lifting the fish completely out of the water until you have it securely in the net.

The Netting Motion – Head First: When you're ready to net the fish, remember that the best approach is head first. Trout are streamlined swimmers, and if you try to scoop them tail-first, they can easily dart away.

- Hold the net low and in position rather than chasing the fish with it.
- Anticipate the right moment—the fish will often glide into the net naturally.
- Use a quick lunge motion with the net, targeting just below the trout's head.

Handling the Trout: Properly handling trout after landing them is one of the most critical aspects of responsible catch-and-release fishing. Trout are incredibly fragile, with delicate slime coats, sensitive gills, and internal organs that can be easily damaged through improper handling. The goal is to minimize stress, injury, and mortality by following best practices that prioritize the trout's well-being. Here's a comprehensive guide to ensure safe and responsible handling:

Keep the Fish in the Water: Trout are aquatic animals and are highly susceptible to the harmful effects of air exposure. Their gills, which are designed to extract oxygen from water, become ineffective when exposed to air. Prolonged air exposure leads to oxygen deprivation, physiological stress, and even death.

Why It Matters: Scientific research indicates that trout exposed to air for more than 30 seconds have significantly reduced survival rates after release. Air exposure of 60 seconds or more can cause permanent physiological damage, reducing the trout's ability to evade predators, forage for food, and recover from the stress of being caught.

Best Practices

Minimize Air Exposure: If you must lift the fish for a photo, limit the exposure to a maximum of 5–10 seconds. A helpful rule is the "Keep Em Wet" principle: keep the fish submerged except for a quick, gentle lift for the photo, and then return it to the water immediately.

Pro Tip: If you notice the trout's gills moving slowly or erratically after air exposure, put the fish into some current and let the waterflow through the gills from the front to reoxygenate its gills.

Wet Your Hands: Trout possess a protective slime coat, also known as the mucous layer, which serves as their first line of defense against bacterial infections, fungal growths, and parasites. Dry hands strip away this layer, leaving the fish vulnerable to disease.

Never Squeeze the Fish: Squeezing a trout to maintain control can cause internal damage, particularly to the heart, liver, and swim bladder.

Pro Tip: If you are struggling to control a fish in order to remove the hook and release it, flip the fish over. This will momentarily disorient the trout, making it easier to handle. Once the hook is removed, gently turn the fish back onto its belly and let the fish swim out of your hand. This simple trick helps reduce stress on the fish and allows for a quicker, safer release.

Best Practices for Safe Hook Removal

Barbless Hooks: Using barbless hooks is a simple but highly effective way to make catch-and-release fishing safer and easier. Not only do they reduce the damage to the fish, but they also make it far easier to remove a hook if you happen to accidentally embed it in your own skin.

Use hemostats or forceps to grip the hook firmly at the bend (not the point) for better control and to avoid injury to the fish. Apply slow, steady pressure to back the hook out along the same path it entered, avoiding any twisting or jerking.

Removing a Hook from Your Skin with Monofilament Line

If you get a hook stuck in your skin and it's not near a sensitive area like your eye, artery, or bone, you can use the monofilament loop method to remove it. Here's how:

Cut the Line – If the hook is still attached to a lure or rod, cut it free so you can work with just the hook.

Press Down on the Eye – Using one hand, firmly press down on the eye of the hook (the loop where the line attaches). This helps disengage the barb.

Loop a Strong Monofilament Line – Take a piece of heavier monofilament (at least 20–30 lb test) and form a loop around the bend of the embedded hook. Could be your leader butt section.

Quick Pull Method – While keeping firm pressure on the hook eye with one hand, use the other to pull the monofilament loop sharply and quickly in the same direction the hook entered. The sudden force will pop the hook out with minimal tissue damage.

Clean and Disinfect – Immediately clean the wound with antiseptic and apply a bandage to prevent infection.

When to Seek Medical Attention

If the hook is near your eye, artery, or bone, do not attempt to remove it. Instead, secure the hook in place (avoid moving it) and go to the emergency room immediately.

16
A Trout's Diet

In order to be a successful fly fisherman, you need to learn about the trout's diet. The trout's most predominant food source is bugs! Leave the Latin for the lovers—you don't need to memorize every insect name to catch fish. Just be able to identify the insect group, match the size, shape, color, and let the trout be your guide.

Entomology: Understanding Insects for Fly Fishing

Entomology, the study of insects, is a game-changer in fly fishing. Knowing what fish eat and when they eat it helps fly fishers pick the right flies and increase their chances of success. Most freshwater fish, especially trout, rely on aquatic insects for food, making them a key focus for fly fishers.

Why Aquatic Insects Matter: Insects like mayflies, caddisflies, stoneflies, and midges are a steady food source for trout. They hatch and transform at predictable times, and fish take advantage. Matching your fly to what's naturally in the water is the best way to fool a fish.

Key Insects for Fly Fishers

Mayflies: A major food source with predictable hatches.

Caddisflies: Hardy insects that hatch in huge numbers.

Stoneflies: Larger meals that trout love, especially in fast water.

Midges: Tiny but essential, especially in winter when few other insects hatch.

Understanding these insects and their life cycles is the key to choosing the right fly at the right time. Master this, and you'll start catching more fish!

Midges (Order: Diptera)

Midges are small, mosquito-like insects that trout feed on year-round, especially in tailwaters and still waters. They hatch consistently, making them a go-to option when other insects aren't active. Midges are the only one of the bug species that come from non-riffle muddy areas of the river. Midges range from the tiny mosquito to the giant cranefly which luckily do not bite.

Midge Life Cycle (4 Stages)

Eggs: Laid on the water's surface, sinking to hatch within days.

Larvae (Annelids): Live in streambed sediment, often cream, red, brown, black, or grey.

Pupae: Rise through the water column, trapped in the surface film becoming emergers.

Adults: Form mating swarms above the water; after laying eggs, they die off.

Fishing Midge Larvae/Pupae (Subsurface Bites!)

Where to Fish: Target slow-moving runs and deeper pools where trout hold and feed, especially areas with steady currents where insects gather. When fishing these spots, let your flies sink to the depths where trout are actively feeding. This approach is particularly effective in places with stable, slower currents, where trout expect an easy meal. This technique excels in tailwaters and deeper sections, as these waters often maintain consistent insect populations throughout the year.

Techniques:

Dead-Drift Nymphing – Keep larvae bouncing along the bottom.

Dropper Rig – Pair a midge larva below a larger attractor nymph or a dry fly.

Greased Leader - Fish an RS2 midge emerger just below the surface.

Pro tip: Let fly rise at the end of the drift.

Top Larva Patterns:

- *Zebra Midge (black, red, olive).*
- *Disco Midge (for red larvae).*
- *Brassie.*

ZEBRA   **DISCO MIDGE**   **BRASSIE**

Top Emerger Patterns:

- *Rojo Midge.*
- *RS2.*

ROJO   RS2

Pro Tip: Use 6X tippet to keep the presentation natural.

Fishing Midge Adults (Surface Action!)

When fishing with dry flies to imitate emerging midges (adult midges), target calm runs and quiet pools, casting gently to rising fish or likely holding spots. Focus particularly on calm areas where midges cluster, such as slower currents or glassy pools. This technique is especially effective during late morning and early afternoon on overcast winter days when trout actively feed at or near the surface.

Techniques:

Dry-Fly Fishing – Best on cloudy days. Use a single midge imitation for rising trout.

Cluster Midge Technique – When trout feed on mating clusters, switch to a larger Griffith's Gnat.

Stick with emergers if you are seeing trout's dorsal fins and tails, change to adults if you see noses breaking the surface.

Top Surface Patterns:

- *Griffith's Gnat (for clusters).*
- *Parachute Midge.*

GRIFFITHS GNAT   **PARACHUTE MIDGE**

Pro Tip: Midges hatch every day of the year. When in doubt you can fish a midge

Common Mistakes & Fixes

Ignoring Pupae → Most trout target midges just before they emerge.
Fishing Too Large → Midges are tiny; use 18–28 size flies.
Dragging Your Fly → A perfect dead drift is critical for success.

Mayflies

Mayflies are slender, delicate insects with upright sailboat like wings and long, wispy tails. Their adult lives are short—sometimes just hours—sometimes a few days, but their hatches bring trout into a feeding frenzy. Small mayflies can be mistaken for midges. Key in on wings.

Life Cycle & Stages: Mayflies go through three key stages:

Nymph – Lives in the water, clings to rocks, and drifts in the current. Trout love these!

Cripple – Not all mayflies hatch perfectly, some will be cripples, and these are the ones can feed on easily.

Dun (Adult) – Emerges at the surface with soft, opaque wings, vulnerable to hungry fish.

Spinner – The final adult form. After mating, they fall to the water in a "spinner fall," an easy meal for trout. You can fool wary trout with spinner imitations like the parachute pheasant tail or rusty spinner, however they are hard to see on the surface.

Why Mayflies Matter in Fly Fishing: Mayflies hatch predictably, based on water temperatures and amount of sunlight. Matching the hatch with the right fly pattern in the correct stag is a must for success.

Top Mayfly Hatches to Know

Blue-Winged Olive (Baetis) – Common emergence spring and fall. Swimming Nymphs.

March Brown (Rhithrogena) – Clinging/Crawling Mayflies. Hatches on sunny days in the spring.

Green and Grey Drake (Ephemera) – A big mayfly trout love in late spring and early summer.

Pale Morning Dun (PMD) – A staple summer mayfly, PMDs hatch or emerge from May to July in the West and June to September in the East. These light yellowish-tan mayflies emerge mid-morning to early afternoon.

Pale Evening Dun - The Pale Evening Dun is a mayfly species that hatches in the late afternoon and evening, making it a prime target for rising trout.

Hexagenia (Brown Drake) – Large, nocturnal hatches that trigger feeding frenzies. Midwest hatch.

Red Quills - Larger mayflies, typically appearing in late summer and early fall.

Tricos are tiny mayflies (sizes 20–26) that hatch in late summer and early fall

Fishing Nymphs (Subsurface): Best early in the hatch or when fish aren't rising. Use dead drift nymphing or Euro nymphing techniques.

Top patterns: Consider these must own. *(#12-18) Pheasant Tail Nymph, Hare's Ear Nymph, Bead Head Prince Nymph.*

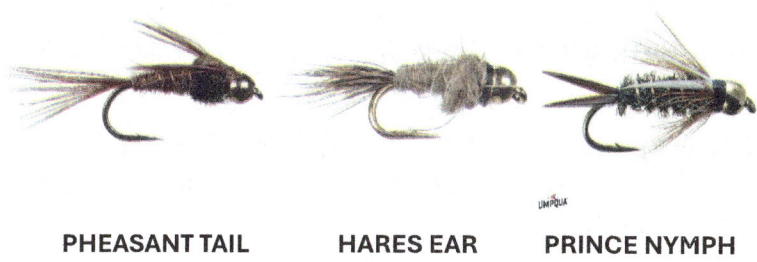

PHEASANT TAIL　　**HARES EAR**　　**PRINCE NYMPH**

Fishing Emergers (Transition Zone): Fish key in on emerging insects stuck in the surface film. You will know fish are eating emergers when you see fins or dorsal fins breaking the surface. Use a greased leader and swinging emerger techniques.

Top patterns: *RS2, Barr's Emerger, Mayfly Cripple.*

RS2　　**PMD EMERGER**　　**CRIPPLE**

Top patterns: *Parachute Adams, Patriot, Para Wulff.* **Fishing**

Duns (Adults): Prime time for dry fly fishing—look for dainty rises. Use dead drift presentations upstream of downstream presentations for picky fish.

PARACHUTE ADAMS   **PATRIOT**   **PARA WULFF**

Fishing Spinners (The Final Stage): Spent mayflies float lifelessly, making an easy meal for trout. Best at dawn or dusk, during a spinner fall.

Top patterns: *Rusty Spinner, Trico Spinner.*

RUSTY SPINNER   **TRICO SPINNER**

Pro Tip: Watch for subtle rise forms—head-and-tail rises often mean trout are eating emergers.

Master the mayfly hatch, and you'll be well on your way to fooling even the pickiest trout!

Common Mistakes & How to Avoid Them

Ignoring Emergers – Even when adults are on the water, fish often feed on cripples and emergers.

Mismatching Size – An off-size fly leads to refusals. Match the hatch closely.

Poor Presentation – Mayflies need a drag-free drift. Use reach casts & mends to eliminate even the slightest drag.

Overlooking Spinner Falls – The best evening dry fly action is often from spinners.

Mayfly hatches bring some of the best fly fishing action. Understanding their life cycle and adapting your approach makes all the difference. Watch water temps, weather, and fish behavior, and match the stage of the insect trout are feeding on. With practice, you'll dial in your strategy and maximize success.

Caddisflies: A Fly Fishing Essential

Caddisflies are among the most abundant aquatic insects, making them a staple food source for trout. They look like small moths, with tent-shaped wings and long antennae. Unlike mayflies, caddisflies lack tails and are strong swimmers and fliers. Their larvae are just as varied—some build protective cases from sand and pebbles, while others are free-living or net-spinning.

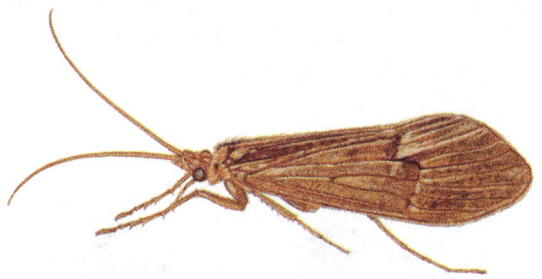

Caddisflies go through complete metamorphosis (egg → larva → pupa → adult), and the pupal stage is the most critical for fly anglers. This is when caddis pupae transform inside protective cases before breaking free and making their rapid ascent to the surface—triggering aggressive trout strikes.

How Pupation Works in Caddisflies

Sealed for Transformation – After feeding as larvae, caddisflies seal themselves inside their cases (made of silk, gravel, or plant debris) and undergo metamorphosis.

Breaking Free – When ready, they chew their way out and begin their rise to the surface, often aided by a gas bubble that gives them buoyancy.

Erratic Swimmers – Unlike mayflies, caddis pupae don't drift passively. They kick, wriggle, and rise quickly toward the film, making them an easy target for trout.

Where to Find Caddisflies: Caddis thrive in fast moving streams and rivers.

Caddisfly Fishing Techniques: Match the Hatch

Caddisflies move erratically—unlike mayflies. Knowing their stages helps you fish them right. Most active when water temperatures are 50-54 degrees.

Fishing Caddis Larvae

Found crawling on streambeds living in rock or stick cases or drifting in currents. Become active just before pupation. Breadcrust nymphs are a perfect imitation.

Best Techniques: Dead Drift Nymphing or Euro Nymphing.

Top Patterns: *Green Rock Worm, Caddis Larva (Olive, Green, Tan), Breadcrust.*

GREEN ROCK WORM   **CADDIS LARVA**   **BREADCRUST**

Pro Tip: Flip stream rocks—match larvae color and size.

Caddis Pupae (The Hatch Trigger)

Pupae rise fast, triggering aggressive strikes. Trout key in on upward movement.

Best Techniques:

Swinging Pupae – Cast across/downstream, let it get down deep in water column and let it swing.

Pro tip: Late in the swing you want to raise your tip and let your fly rise to the surface.

Indicator Nymphing – Drift with subtle twitches.

Top Patterns: *Emerging Sparkle Pupa, Soft Hackle Caddis Pupa, Deep Sparkle Pupa, Bubble Caddis.*

SPARKLE PUPA   **SOFT HACKLE**   **BUBBLE CADDIS**

Pro Tip: Use flashy patterns to mimic gas bubbles.

Fishing Adult Caddisflies (Surface Action!)

Caddis skitter and bounce—dead drifts aren't always enough.

Best Techniques:

Dead Drift – When adults rest, let it float naturally.

Skitter, Skate or Dance – Twitch rod tip to mimic egg-laying. You do not want to drag.

Emerger Technique – At the end of your drift, do not just take fly out of water to cast. Slowly lift it imitating an emerging caddis. You will frequently get strikes on the lift.

Top Patterns: *Elk Hair Caddis, Goddard Caddis, X-Caddis. Stimulator.*

ELK HAIR CADDIS   **GODDARD CADDIS**   **X CADDIS**

Common Mistakes and How to Avoid Them

Ignoring Pupa Activity – Many anglers focus on adults, but trout often prefer pupae.

Mistaking Rises for Surface Feeding - Adult Caddisflies leave the surface quickly. Mistaking rises for trout feeding on the surface when in fact they are feeding on the emergers underneath the surface and their momentum carries them out of the water.

Over-Mending the Line – Too much mending unnaturally moves the fly—gentle twitches work better.

Mismatched Size & Color – Caddisflies vary widely—carry multiple sizes and colors.

Fishing Only Dead Drifts – Caddisflies skitter and flutter—add movement for more strikes.

Caddis hatches are the predominant insect and food source for trout in the western U.S. and bring aggressive feeding, making them some of the most exciting dry fly opportunities. Learn to fish each stage, watch fish behavior, and adapt to conditions. The more you understand the hatch, the more fish you'll land!

Stoneflies

Stoneflies are among the most protein-rich meals a trout can find, making them a prized food source throughout their life cycle. They prefer well-oxygenated, fast-moving waters with rocky bottoms, where they cling to stones and debris. Unlike other aquatic insects that hatch in a matter of months, some species of stoneflies, such as the large Pteronarcys (Salmon flies), can spend up to three years in the nymph stage before emerging. This extended development period means there are always stonefly nymphs available for opportunistic trout to feed on, especially when they shed their exoskeletons allowing for growth to occur and making them vulnerable for trout.

Stonefly Life Cycle (3 Stages)

Eggs: Laid in clusters on the water's surface, sinking to rocks below.

Nymphs: Live 1-3 years under rocks, growing large up to size (#2-4).

Adults: Short-lived, focused on mating and egg-laying, often in the late afternoon.

Stoneflies thrive in cold, oxygen-rich rivers, often found in stone-lined canyons where fast currents and rocky substrates provide the perfect habitat. These rugged environments, with their churning waters and deep pools, offer ideal conditions for stonefly nymphs to cling to submerged rocks and boulders as they grow. Their long nymphal stage—sometimes lasting up to three years—ensures a consistent food source for trout year-round.

Salmon Flies

Salmon flies (Pteronarcys) tend to hatch in late spring to early summer, when water temperatures reach the mid-50s. This emergence often coincides with high water and potentially off colored water from snowmelt, making it one of the most exciting and anticipated hatches of the year, but can also be inconsistent on certain rivers that are not dam controlled. Trout gorge themselves on these massive insects, sometimes becoming so full they can barely swim. The best fishing often happens along grassy banks, where adult salmon flies crawl onto land to dry their wings, before taking flight—or falling clumsily into the river, becoming easy prey.

Top Patterns: *Black/Brown K Stone, Rogue River Stone*

BLACK STONE   BROWN STONE   ROGUE RIVER STONE

Yellow Sallies

As summer progresses, Yellow Sallies (Isoperla) make their appearance, hatching primarily in mid-morning. These small, bright yellow stoneflies are much more delicate than salmon flies or golden stones, but trout still love them. They tend to emerge on warm mid-summer days, popping out of the water, similar to a caddis fly.

Top Patterns: *Sponge Bob, Copper Bead Poxy Back Biot Golden Stone*

SPONGE BOB   BIOT GOLDEN STONE

Yes, there is a Small Green Stonefly, commonly known as the Green Sally. These small, vibrant green stoneflies tend to hatch around the same time as Yellow Sallies, usually in mid to late summer. Try green Prince Nymphs.

Giant Golden Stoneflies

Giant Golden Stoneflies emerge slightly later, hatching in mid to late summer, often at night or during early, rainy mornings. Their hatch is less chaotic than the salmon fly emergence, but trout still take notice.

Top Patterns: *Pat's Rubber Legs, Chubby Chernobyl*

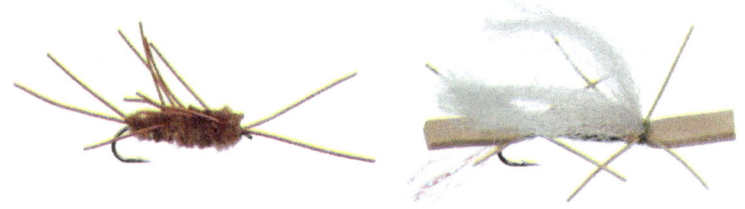

PAT'S RUBBER LEGS   **CHUBBY CHERNOBYL**

Common Mistakes & Fixes

Ignoring the Shoreline → Concentrate of steep rocky shorelines.

Presenting Too Gently → Stoneflies land with a plop!

Fishing Too High in the Water Column → Get nymphs deep.

Using the Wrong Size → Match the hatch!

Terrestrials

Terrestrial insects—grasshoppers, ants, beetles, crickets, and cicadas—become key trout food sources in late spring, summer, and early fall. Unlike aquatic insects, terrestrials fall into the water unpredictably, triggering aggressive strikes.

Grasshoppers: The Splashy Plunge

Best Time: Mid-to-late summer, especially on windy afternoons.

Where to Fish: Along grassy banks, undercut banks, and near meadows.

Top Pattern: *Morning Wood Hopper Craven Yellow*

Pro Tip: Early season hoppers are more green, late season hoppers are darker, more brown and black.

Ants (M & M Candy for Trout)

Best Time: Warm, sunny days; peak activity in late summer.

Where to Fish: Under overhanging trees and near grassy banks.

Pro tip: In the western states, we frequently get swarms of fly ants. Watch for aggressive rises if you see no obvious hatches occurring. This can be an indication trout are feeding on ants.

Top Pattern: *Parachute Ant*

Beetles & Crickets (The Unexpected Meal)

Best Time: Late spring through early fall, especially on windy days.

Where to Fish: Shady banks, under trees, and along grassy shorelines.

Top Pattern: Hi Vis Beetle

Pro Tip: On small creeks cast a foam beetle near undercut banks.

Fishing crickets on streams is an exciting and effective way to entice trout, especially in late summer when these terrestrial insects often fall into the water. Their frantic struggle on the surface triggers aggressive strikes from opportunistic fish.

Top Pattern: Big Secret Ho Cricket

Natural Prey: Mimicking the Trout's Menu

Success on the fly begins with understanding what your target is feeding on. In many freshwater systems, trout are enticed by a variety of small, natural organisms.

Crawdads (Crayfish)

Crawdads are common along stream beds, often hiding under rocks. Their distinctive, clawed movements and segmented bodies are a favorite for trout.

Top Pattern: *Woolly Bugger Rust Color*

Sculpins

Sculpins are bottom dwellers with a rough, mottled texture. They move slowly along the substrate, making them a natural target. Try Black, Brown or Olive.

Top Pattern: *Woolly Buggers Rust and Brown*

Minnows

Agile and quick, minnows add dynamic movement to the trout's diet.

Top Pattern: *Murdich Mini Minnow*

Small Trout Fry

Although less common, small trout fry are a natural part of the food chain.

Top Pattern: *Dirty Hippie Rainbow Trout*

Leeches

Leeches are slender, segmented creatures that glide slowly through the water. Their undulating motion is particularly enticing to trout.

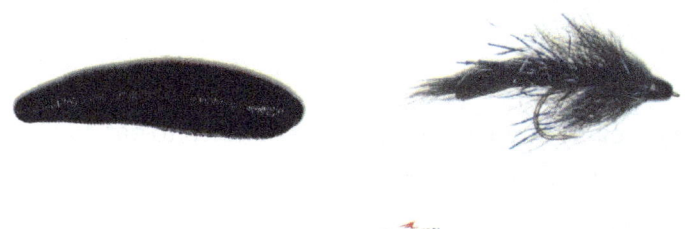

Top Pattern: *Lightning Leech*

Fish Eggs

During spawning seasons, fish eggs provide another visual cue for trout. Their clustered, delicate appearance has inspired many fly designs.

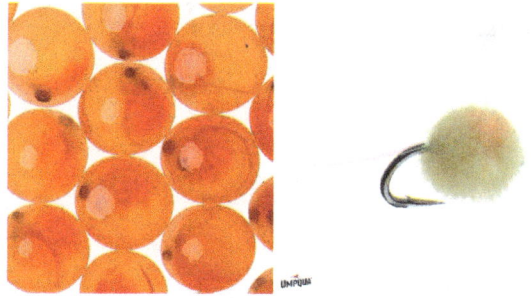

Top Pattern: *Flash Tail Egg Various Colors and Sizes*

Aquatic Worms

Wriggling aquatic worms—such as bloodworms—are another favorite. Their constant, lively movement makes them excellent models for fly patterns.

Top Pattern: *San Juan Flash Worm Various Colors and Sizes*

Mice

Trout, especially larger ones have been known to eat a mouse that inadvertently falls into the water.

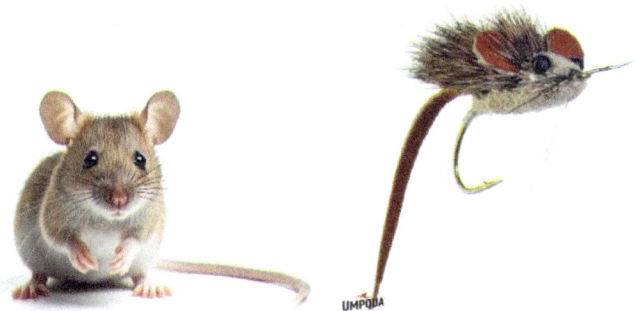

Top Pattern: *Mini Mouse*

17
Trout Identification

Trout are among the most sought-after fish in freshwater angling, prized for their beauty, behavior, and challenge to catch. While there are many species of trout, four of the most commonly encountered are Rainbow Trout, Brown Trout, Brook Trout, and Cutthroat Trout. Proper identification is essential for anglers, especially in areas with species-specific regulations and conservation efforts.

Rainbow Trout (Oncorhynchus mykiss)

Appearance: Rainbow trout are easily recognized by their shimmering, silvery bodies adorned with small black spots and a pinkish-red stripe running along their sides. Their coloration varies depending on habitat and spawning season.

Key Features:

- Pink to red lateral stripe.
- Black spots on dorsal fin, tail, and upper body.
- Silvery body, turning darker during spawning.

Habitat: Native to the Pacific drainages of North America but introduced worldwide. Found in cold, clear rivers, streams, and lakes.

Diet and Behavior: Rainbow trout are opportunistic feeders, consuming insects, crustaceans, and small fish. They are known for their acrobatic jumps when hooked, making them a favorite among anglers.

Spawning: Typically spawn in spring when water temperatures reach 42-44°F. Females dig nests, or redds, in gravel beds where eggs are deposited and fertilized.

Brown Trout (Salmo trutta)

Appearance: Brown trout typically have golden-brown bodies with black, red, and orange spots, often encircled by light halos.

Key Features:

- Golden-brown coloration.
- Black and red spots with pale halos.
- Squared-off tail.

Habitat: Native to Europe, brown trout have been introduced to North America and thrive in cold, oxygen-rich waters. Found in streams, rivers, and lakes.

Diet and Behavior: Brown trout are nocturnal feeders, primarily consuming insects, crustaceans, and small fish. Larger individuals may become piscivorous, preying on other fish.

Spawning: Spawn in autumn, digging redds in gravelly streams. Eggs develop over winter and hatch in spring.

Brook Trout (Salvelinus fontinalis) *(Technically a char)*

Appearance: Brook trout have dark green to brown bodies with a marbled pattern, known as vermiculation, along the back and dorsal fin. Their lower fins have white leading edges with black lines.

Key Features:

- Dark, worm-like patterns on back.
- Pale spots on a dark background.
- White-bordered fins with black stripes.

Habitat: Native to eastern North America but introduced across the continent. Prefers cool, clear, spring-fed streams and lakes.

Diet and Behavior: Brook trout feed on aquatic and terrestrial insects, small fish, and crustaceans. They are more active in cooler temperatures and are often found in higher-elevation streams.

Spawning: Spawn in fall in cold, well-oxygenated streams with gravel substrates.

Cutthroat Trout (Oncorhynchus clarkii)

Appearance: Named for the distinctive red or orange slash marks under the jaw, cutthroat trout vary in color from golden yellow to silvery gray.

Key Features:

- Red or orange slashes under the jaw.
- Small black spots, more concentrated toward the tail.
- Yellowish to olive body.

Habitat: Native to western North America, cutthroat trout inhabit rivers, streams, and lakes, with several distinct subspecies adapted to specific watersheds.

Diet and Behavior: Primarily feed on aquatic and terrestrial insects but will consume small fish and crustaceans. Their feeding behavior varies by subspecies and habitat.

Spawning: Spring spawners, with exact timing depending on elevation and water temperature. Redds are typically dug in gravelly streambeds.

18
Conclusion

Fly fishing is a beautiful blend of skill, patience, and respect for nature—a rewarding pursuit for those who embrace learning, adaptation, and the subtle mysteries of the water. Throughout this book, you've gained a solid foundation in fly fishing, from selecting essential gear and mastering basic knots, to understanding trout behavior, refining your casting techniques and choosing the right flies to match the hatch. But your journey doesn't end here. Continue expanding your knowledge on advanced fly casting methods, the nuances of reading streams, specialized knots, detailed fly tying techniques, and deeper insights into effectively fishing dry flies, nymphs, and streamers.

To further enhance your skills, consider exploring the multitude of excellent fly fishing books available, diving into online instructional resources, attending casting clinics, enrolling in college courses, or even going on guided fishing trips. Joining clubs or organizations such as your local Trout Unlimited chapter or other conservation-focused groups can connect you with passionate anglers dedicated to protecting rivers and trout habitats. Fishing alongside experienced fly fishers provides invaluable firsthand learning opportunities, while regularly visiting your local fly shops offers expert advice and the latest insights on gear and river conditions.

As you step into the water, keep in mind that fly fishing is ultimately about connection: to the river, to the fish, and to yourself. So, fish responsibly, never stop learning, and savor every moment spent on the river.

19
About the Authors & Map the Xperience

Bill Perry

Bill is a partner at Map the Xperience and a former owner/operator of Fly Fishing Outfitters, a business he successfully ran for over two decades. After selling the fly shop in 2008, he transitioned to part-time guiding, continuing to share his expertise on the water.

A highly accomplished angler, Bill is a member of the Freshwater Fisheries Hall of Fame, an IGFA world record holder for Kokanee Salmon in the South Platte River, a four-time Colorado Master Angler, and a two-time Orvis Outfitter of the Year. He also served as a professor of fly fishing at Colorado Mountain College for over a decade, teaching the accredited Fly Fishing 101 course every spring and fall.

As a founding board member of the Eagle River Coalition, Bill has long been dedicated to conservation and education in the fly-fishing community. Since the early '90s, he has specialized in guide training schools and rowing certification programs, accumulating over 20,000 commercial river miles as a guide and trainer.

Between 2009 and 2018, Bill worked with Vail Valley Anglers as a resort marketing specialist, content writer, guide trainer, and professional guide. When he's not marketing map products or writing books, he leads private rowing schools and float trips on the Eagle and Colorado Rivers for Colorado Angling Company, a team of expert guides based in a riverside cabin in Wolcott, Colorado.

A graduate of St. Michael's College in Vermont, Bill is often referred to as a "guide's guide." He has led trips for renowned anglers, from John Barr to Flip Pallot, and his fly patterns have been featured in Orvis and on the cover of *Fly Tying Magazine*. A two-time champion of the Eagle Valley Fall Fly Fishing Classic, he remains an active member of the Eagle Valley Chapter of Trout Unlimited.

Daniel Bryant

Dan is our avid fly fisherman, hiker and hunter extraordinaire. He brings a wealth of knowledge from his experiences and supplies the maps with hands-on information that makes these maps a must-have. Residing in Colorado for most of his life, Dan has climbed many peaks and endured trips where survival tactics were required. Dan studied Business and Economics before becoming General Manager of Orvis Fly Fishing

Outfitters for 12 years. Dan has fly fished for almost 50 years. He guided in Alaska where he survived a harrowing Grizzly Bear attack. Dan knows what useful information the typical outdoorsman wants on a map because he is the true outdoorsman. Dan has been instrumental in the map creation providing the data and expertise that makes these maps one of kind masterpieces. Dan also created the Handy Map Microfiber Cloth Bandana sold in national parks and specialty retailers nationwide.

Greg Tanaka

Greg is a partner in Map the Xperience and our map guru. He creates our maps and designs them to be intuitive, easy to navigate and beautiful to look at. Previously, he spent several years creating Harley Davidson's series of motorcycle ride maps. Some of his earlier works have been inducted in to the Library of Congress. He has earned 4 map awards and 3 design awards for his past works. A lifelong Californian who resides in the SF Bay area, Greg's passion now is to teach his kids the art of fishing and to appreciate the beautiful outdoors.

Fly Fishing Terminology

A

Acceleration – The gradual increase in speed during the casting stroke, essential for smooth and controlled casting.

Accuracy – The ability to deliver the fly to a precise location on the water, crucial for effective fly presentation.

Action – The flexibility of a fly rod, determining how it bends and casts.

Aerial Mend – A technique used to reposition the fly line while it is still in the air before it lands on the water, reducing drag and improving drift.

AFFTA (American Fly-Fishing Trade Association) – The organization that standardizes fly line weights for consistency across manufacturers.

Albright Knot – A knot used to connect backing to fly line, ensuring a strong and smooth transition.

Anchor Fly – The heaviest fly in a multi-nymph rig, used to help the setup sink quickly to the riverbed.

Aerosol Floatant – A spray-based floatant used for treating multiple flies quickly and efficiently.

Arbor – The center part of a fly reel where the backing and fly line are wound.

Arbor Knot – A knot used to secure backing to the reel, preventing slippage.

B

Back cast – The backward motion of a fly rod during casting.

Backing – A thin, strong braided line that sits beneath the fly line, increasing reel capacity and providing extra length for fish that make long runs.

Balance – The relationship between the weight of the rod and reel to ensure comfortable casting and reduce fatigue.

Base Layers – Moisture-wicking clothing worn against the skin to regulate temperature.

Bass Leaders – Leaders designed for targeting bass, typically stiffer to handle large flies.

Belly (D-Loop) – The loop of line that forms behind the rod in a roll cast, providing the necessary energy to propel the line forward.

Blank – The main body of the fly rod, typically constructed from high-modulus graphite for strength and flexibility.

Blood Knot – A strong, streamlined knot used to join two pieces of similar diameter line.

Bonefish & Permit Lines – Fly lines designed for saltwater flats species, featuring stiff cores and tropical coatings to withstand heat.

Bow and Arrow Cast – A specialized casting technique where the angler holds the fly and bends the rod like a bow before releasing to propel the fly forward, useful in tight spaces with little back casting room.

Breathable Waders – Waterproof pants that allow sweat to escape while keeping the wearer dry.

C

Casting Arc – The range of motion the rod travels during a cast, typically between the 10 o'clock and 1 o'clock positions.

Casting Stroke – The movement of the rod during the cast, from the start of acceleration to the abrupt stop.

CNC Machining – A precision manufacturing process where reels are cut from solid aluminum blocks using Computer Numerical Control (CNC) technology for enhanced durability and strength.

Click-and-Pawl Drag – A simple, mechanical drag system using a ratchet-and-spring design to create light resistance when line is pulled off the reel.

Clinch Knot (Improved Clinch Knot) – A common knot used to tie a fly to the tippet, also called a fisherman's knot.

Cold Water Fly Lines – Fly lines made with softer, flexible coatings that prevent stiffness in cold conditions, used for trout, steelhead, and salmon fishing.

Compartment Plastic Boxes – Storage boxes with separate

compartments for organizing larger flies.

Composite Reels – Fly reels made from plastic or composite materials, often lightweight but less durable compared to aluminum reels.

Conehead Streamer – A streamer fly with a weighted cone-shaped head, designed to help it sink and mimic baitfish.

Corrosion Resistance – The ability of a reel material (e.g., anodized aluminum) to resist rust and damage from saltwater environments.

Czech Nymphing – A fly-fishing technique that uses a tight-line approach with multiple weighted nymphs to fish close to the riverbed.

Current Speed – The velocity of the water flow, which affects the fly's drift and how mends need to be applied.

D

Dacron Backing – A common fly line backing made of synthetic fiber, available in 20-30 lb. test ratings, known for reliability and affordability.

Dapping – A technique where the fly is repeatedly bounced or "dapped" on the water's surface to mimic an insect, often used in small streams or for dry fly fishing.

Death Grip Syndrome – A common beginner mistake where the angler grips the fly rod too tightly, leading to poor casting mechanics.

Desiccant – A drying powder used to restore buoyancy to waterlogged dry flies.

Die-Cast Reels – Fly reels made by casting molten aluminum into a mold rather than machining. These are more affordable but generally less durable.

Disc Drag System – A modern fly reel drag system that uses carbon, cork, or ceramic discs to create adjustable friction, providing smooth and consistent stopping power.

Double Dry Fly Rig – A rigging method where two dry flies are used to mimic multiple hatching insects.

Double Haul – A casting technique where the angler pulls (hauls) on the fly line during both the back and forward cast to increase line speed and casting distance.

Double Nymph Rig – A fly-fishing setup using two nymphs at different depths to increase the chance of catching fish.

Double Reach Cast – A variation of the reach cast that adds an extra reach in both the back and forward casts to improve line placement and reduce drag.

Double Taper (DT) Line – A fly line tapered at both ends, providing smooth, delicate presentations and allowing reversal for extended use.

Downstream – Casting or positioning oneself in the direction that the water is flowing toward.

Drag – The unnatural movement of a fly caused by tension between the fly line and the current, which can cause fish to reject the fly.

Drag-Free Drift – A fly presentation where the fly moves naturally with the current.

Drag System – The internal mechanism of a fly reel that controls how much resistance is applied when line is pulled off the spool, crucial for fighting fish.

Drift – The natural motion of the fly as it moves with the current after the cast.

Drop Cast – A technique where the fly is allowed to settle softly on the water to avoid spooking fish.

Dropper Fly – A secondary fly tied behind the first fly, often used in double fly rigs.

Dropper Loop – A loop in the leader or tippet that allows for attaching an additional fly.

Dry Fly – A type of fly designed to float on the water's surface, mimicking adult insects.

Dry Fly Dropper Rig (Hopper-Dropper) – A hybrid rig where a dry fly acts as a strike indicator while a nymph or emerger is suspended below.

Dry Shake – A desiccant powder applied to dry flies to absorb moisture and restore floatation.

Duncan Loop (Uni Knot) – A versatile knot used to attach a fly to the tippet, allowing for enhanced movement in the water.

E

Emerger – A type of fly that imitates an insect in the process of transitioning from a nymph to an adult.

Euro Nymphing Lines – Ultra-thin, low-stretch lines designed for increased sensitivity and control in tight-line nymphing techniques.

Euro Nymphing Leaders – Extra-long leaders optimized for sensitivity and direct contact when fishing nymphs.

F

False Cast – A series of back-and-forth overhead casts where the line remains in the air without landing on the water, used for drying a fly, changing direction, or adjusting distance.

Ferrules – Connection points where multi-piece rod sections fit together, allowing for portability and balanced performance.

Fiberglass Fly Rods – An alternative to graphite rods, offering slower action, durability, and a nostalgic casting experience.

Fishing Vest – A garment with multiple pockets for carrying fly fishing gear.

Float Line – A type of fly line designed to remain on the surface of the water, commonly used for most freshwater fly fishing applications.

Floatant – A substance applied to dry flies to help them stay buoyant on the water's surface.

Floating Fly Line – A fly line that stays on the water's surface, used primarily for dry fly fishing.

Floating Line (F) – A fly line that stays on the surface, ideal for dry flies, nymphing, and general trout and bass fishing.

Fluorocarbon Tippet – A nearly invisible and abrasion-resistant tippet material that sinks quickly, ideal for nymphs and streamers.

Fly Box – A protective container designed to hold and organize artificial flies.

Fly Dip – A liquid floatant used to coat dry flies and extend their buoyancy.

Fly Fishing Weights – Various weights such as split shot,

tungsten putty, and lead to help flies sink to the desired depth.

Fly Line – The weighted, coated line used in fly fishing to cast flies effectively.

Fly Line Length – The total length of a fly line, typically ranging from 80 to 120 feet, with standard trout lines measuring 90 feet.

Fly Line Memory – The tendency of fly line to retain coiled loops when stored on a reel with a small arbor.

Fly Line Nomenclature – The labeling system used to describe fly line characteristics, including taper type, weight, and sink rate (e.g., WF-6-F/S).

Fly Line Taper – The distribution of weight along the fly line, affecting casting ability and presentation. Common tapers include Weight Forward (WF), Double Taper (DT), Shooting Taper (ST), and Triangle Taper (TT).

Fly Line Weight – The standardized weight of a fly line, ranging from 1-weight (very light) to 15-weight (very heavy), which must be matched to a fly rod for proper performance.

Fly Reel – A device attached to the rod used for storing and managing fly line.

Fly Rod Weights – Classification of fly rods based on the weight of the fly line they are designed to cast, ranging from 1 to 15 weight.

Foam Boxes – Lightweight fly storage boxes with slotted foam to secure flies.

Foam Strike Indicator – A buoyant, adjustable indicator used to detect subtle strikes while nymphing.

Follow-Through – The final motion of a cast where the rod tip is directed toward the target, ensuring accuracy and a clean presentation.

Forward Cast – The portion of the fly cast where the line is propelled toward the target.

Full-Sinking Line (S) – A fly line that sinks at a consistent rate, used for deepwater fishing in lakes and reservoirs.

G

Gel Floatant – A waterproofing solution applied to dry flies before fishing to enhance buoyancy.
Gel-Spun Backing – A high-capacity backing made from polyethylene fibers, offering greater strength and abrasion resistance than Dacron.
Grip – The handle of a fly rod, usually made of cork.
Grip Pressure – The amount of force applied to the rod handle; too much pressure reduces flexibility and casting accuracy, while too little can cause instability.
Gravel Guards – Protective covers attached to waders to keep sand and debris out of boots.
Guide – The small loops along a fly rod that guide the line during casting and retrieval.
Improved Clinch Knot – A knot used to attach the fly to the tippet, offering a secure hold.

H

Hand-Tied Leaders – Leaders constructed by tying sections of different diameters together for customized setups.
Haul – A short, quick pull on the fly line to increase line speed, typically used in a double haul.
Hard-Anodized Aluminum – A protective treatment applied to aluminum reels to increase corrosion resistance and durability, especially for saltwater use.
Hemostats (Forceps) – A clamp-like tool used to remove hooks from fish.

I

Improved Clinch Knot – A knot used to attach the fly to the tippet, offering a secure hold.
Indicator – A device (foam, yarn, or other materials) attached to the leader to help detect when a fish strikes the fly.
Intermediate Sink Line (I) – A fly line that sinks slowly (1-2 inches per second), commonly used in still water fishing.
Insulating Layer – A layer of clothing designed to trap body heat while allowing moisture to escape.

K

Knotless Tapered Leaders – Leaders manufactured as a single piece with a smooth taper, offering seamless energy transfer.

L

Large Arbor Reel – A reel with a wider spool diameter, allowing for faster line retrieval and reduced fly line memory.

Leader – A tapered section of monofilament or fluorocarbon that connects the fly line to the tippet, ensuring a natural drift.

Lead Split Shot – Small, crimpable lead weights used to sink nymphs in fast-moving water.

Level Line (L) – A fly line without taper, primarily used in specialty applications.

Line Capacity – The amount of fly line and backing a reel can hold, typically measured in yards and influenced by the reel's arbor size.

Line Control – The ability to manage slack, mend, and manipulate the fly line for a controlled and precise presentation.

Line Slap – When the fly line hits the water or rod too early due to poor timing or excessive force.

Loop Formation – The shape of the fly line as it travels through the air during the cast. A tight loop is more efficient, while a wide loop loses energy and control.

Loop Knot (Non-Slip Loop Knot) – A knot that provides increased movement for flies in the water.

Loop-to-Loop Connection – A method of connecting a leader to the fly line using interlocking loops for easy rigging.

M

Machined Reel – A fly reel created from a single block of aluminum using CNC technology, making it stronger, lighter, and more precise than stamped reels.

Magnetic Glasses – Flip-down magnifiers used to assist with fly tying.

Major Fly Line Manufacturers – Companies that produce

high-quality fly lines, including RIO Products, Scientific Anglers, Airflo, and Cortland.

Mayflies, Caddisflies, Stoneflies – Common aquatic insects that serve as a primary food source for trout.

Mending – The act of repositioning the fly line on the water after a cast to eliminate drag and improve drift.

Merino Wool – A natural fiber known for its moisture-wicking and temperature-regulating properties.

Monofilament – A single-strand fishing line material commonly used for leaders and tippets.

Monofilament Tippet – A flexible, buoyant material used for dry fly presentations.

Multi-Piece Construction – Modern rods are designed in sections for easy transport and storage, commonly available in four-piece configurations.

N

Nail Knot – A knot used to attach the leader to the fly line, often replaced by loop-to-loop connections.

Natural Drift – A drift in which the fly moves exactly like a natural insect without drag.

Neck Gaiters (Buffs) – Fabric tubes worn around the neck and face for sun, wind, and insect protection.

Neutral Wrist – A relaxed wrist position in line with the forearm, helping to maintain smooth and controlled casting movements.

Nippers – Small cutting tools used to trim fishing line and tippet material.

Non-Slip Loop Knot – A knot that creates a loop at the end of the line, allowing for more fly movement.

Nymph – A subsurface fly that mimics the immature stage of aquatic insects.

Nymph Rig – A setup designed for fishing nymphs below the water's surface.

Nymphing – A fly fishing technique that involves using underwater flies (nymphs) to imitate aquatic insects.

O

Open Loops – A wide, inefficient loop in a fly cast that loses energy and accuracy, often caused by an excessive casting stroke or too much wrist movement.

Outer Shell Layer – A waterproof and windproof jacket worn to protect against the elements.

Overhand Loop – A simple knot used to create a loop in the leader or tippet, often used for attaching weights.

Overhead Cast – The most fundamental fly casting technique involving a back cast followed by a forward cast to deliver the fly to the target.

P

Pause – A momentary stop between the back cast and forward cast to allow the fly line to fully extend before beginning the next motion.

Pick-Up and Lay Down Cast (PULD) – A simple casting technique where the fly is lifted from the water and then laid back down in a controlled manner.

Pike & Musky Lines – Fly lines designed for casting oversized streamers, often featuring built-in sink tips and aggressive tapers.

Pocket Water – Small, turbulent sections of a river where fish often hold.

Polarized Sunglasses – Eyewear that reduces water glare and enhances underwater visibility.

Power Application – The controlled acceleration and abrupt stop of the fly rod that transfers energy into the fly line.

Presentation – The way a fly is delivered and behaves in the water to appear natural to fish.

Puddle Cast – A casting technique where extra slack is introduced into the line to allow the fly to drift naturally in currents with minimal drag.

Q

Quick-Release Spool – A reel feature allowing anglers to easily swap out different fly lines without dismantling the entire reel.

R

Reach Cast – A casting technique where the angler extends the rod to one side before the line lands, helping to reduce drag in complex currents.
Rear Grip – A grip position where the angler holds the rod farther back for more leverage on longer casts.
Reading the River – The skill of identifying productive fishing spots by observing current patterns and structure.
Reel Seat – The component that secures the fly reel to the rod, ensuring stability during use.
Rod Action – Describes how much a rod bends when casting.
Rod Length – Fly rods typically range from 7 to 10 feet, with different lengths suited for various fishing environments.
Rod Loading – The bending of the rod caused by the weight of the fly line, which stores and then releases energy during the cast.
Roll Cast – A casting technique that eliminates the need for a back cast by using the tension of the water to load the rod and propel the fly line forward.
Rubber Nets – Fish-friendly landing nets that minimize harm to fish during catch-and-release.
Rubber Soled Boots – Footwear designed to provide traction on various terrains, often featuring Vibram soles.

S

Sealed Drag System – A drag system enclosed to prevent dirt, sand, and water from interfering with performance, ideal for saltwater and extreme conditions.
Saltwater Reel – A fly reel specifically designed with corrosion-resistant materials, sealed drag systems, and durability for use in saltwater environments.
Shooting Head – A short, heavy front section of a fly line

designed for long-distance casting, commonly used in saltwater and Spey fishing.

Shooting Line – Releasing additional fly line through the guides during a cast to increase casting distance.

Shock Mending – A sudden, forceful mend applied to the line immediately after the cast to counteract strong currents.

Sink Rate – The speed at which a sinking fly line descends in water, measured in inches per second (IPS). Categories include Floating (0 IPS), Intermediate Sink (1-2 IPS), Slow Sink (3-4 IPS), Medium Sink (5-6 IPS), and Fast Sink (7-8+ IPS).

Sink Tip Line (F/S) – A fly line with a floating main section and a sinking tip, used for presenting flies deeper while maintaining line control.

Sighter – A high-visibility section of monofilament used in tight-line nymphing to detect subtle strikes.

Single Dry Fly Rig – The most basic fly-fishing setup, using one dry fly.

Single Nymph Rig – A rig designed to fish one nymph subsurface.

Slack Line – Extra or loose line that can interfere with casting accuracy and control.

Specialty Species-Specific Fly Lines – Fly lines designed with specific fish species in mind, featuring specialized tapers, coatings, and weight distributions to optimize performance.

Spey Casting – A two-handed casting technique used in large rivers for steelhead and salmon fishing, often requiring specialty long-head fly lines.

Split Shot – Small weights added to the leader to help nymphs sink to the desired depth.

Stack Mending – A method of repeatedly mending the line to add slack, allowing for an extended drift.

Stamped Reel – A fly reel made by stamping or molding aluminum rather than machining, often more affordable but less durable.

Steelhead & Salmon Lines – Fly lines designed for anadromous fish species, often featuring long heads for smooth mending and Spey casting.

Stick-On Indicator – A lightweight adhesive indicator for delicate presentations and shallow water fishing.
Stop and Pop – A quick and firm stop at the end of the casting stroke, transferring energy from the rod into the line.
Streamer – A type of fly that imitates baitfish, leeches, or other swimming prey.
Streamer Rig – A setup designed for fishing large flies that mimic baitfish.
Strike Indicator – A device used to signal when a fish has taken the fly, functioning similarly to a bobber in conventional fishing.
Studded Soles – Footwear soles with embedded metal studs for improved traction in slippery conditions.
Sun Hoodie – A lightweight, long-sleeved shirt with UPF-rated fabric for sun protection.
Surgeon's Knot – A quick and strong knot used to connect tippet to leader.

T

Target Species – The type of fish an angler is pursuing, which influences reel selection based on required drag strength, backing capacity, and durability.
Tailing Loop – A casting error where the top and bottom parts of the fly line cross, often caused by improper acceleration or excessive wrist movement.
Tapered Leader – A leader with a thick butt section that gradually decreases in diameter to facilitate a smooth energy transfer.
Tenkara Rods – A traditional Japanese fly rod style with no reel, used for small stream fishing with a fixed-length line.
Thumb-on-Top Grip – The most common fly rod grip where the thumb is placed along the top of the cork handle for better control and power.
Tight Loops – A narrow, efficient loop in the fly line that results in better energy transfer, accuracy, and distance.
Tight-Line Nymphing – A method of fishing nymphs without a strike indicator, keeping direct contact with the flies.

Timing – The coordination of movements between the back cast, pause, and forward cast to ensure proper energy transfer and loop formation.
Tippet – The final, thinnest section of the leader to which the fly is tied, ensuring a natural presentation.
Tippet Holder – A small device that organizes and dispenses different sizes of tippet material.
Tippet Rings – Small metal rings used to connect leader and tippet, reducing waste and making tippet replacement easier.
Tippet Size – A rating system (X-System) determining the diameter and strength of tippet material.
Tippet Spool Organizer – A tool that holds multiple tippet spools for easy access.
Tracking – Keeping the rod tip moving in a straight line during the casting stroke to improve accuracy and loop control.
Triangle Taper (TT) Line – A variation of a weight-forward taper, ideal for roll casting and delicate presentations.
Trout Stream – A flowing water body that provides habitat for trout, often characterized by riffles, pools, and runs.
Trout-Specific Fly Lines – Fly lines tailored for trout fishing, often featuring soft tapers for delicate dry fly presentations and textured coatings for better floatation.
Turnover – The point in the cast where the fly line, leader, and fly fully extend before landing on the water.
Tungsten Putty – A moldable, reusable weight that can be adjusted for fine-tuning depth.
Tungsten Weight – A denser alternative to lead, used to sink flies quickly with less bulk.

U

Upstream Presentation – Casting the fly upstream and allowing it to drift naturally toward the angler.

W

Wading Belt – A belt worn over waders to enhance safety and reduce water intake if submerged.
Wading Boots – Specialized footwear designed for traction

and stability in rivers and streams.

Wading Staff – A collapsible walking stick that provides balance and support while wading.

Warm Water Fly Lines – Fly lines with stiffer coatings designed for bass, pike, and saltwater species in hot climates, preventing limpness in warm temperatures.

Waterproof Fly Boxes – Protective cases designed to keep flies dry in wet conditions.

Weight Forward (WF) Line – The most common fly line taper, featuring extra weight at the front to aid casting distance and ease of use.

Weight Matching – The practice of pairing a fly reel's weight with the appropriate fly rod weight (e.g., a 5-weight reel with a 5-weight rod) for optimal performance.

Weighted Nymph – A nymph fly with added weight (such as a bead head) to help it sink.

Wet Fly – A fly that is designed to be fished beneath the surface, imitating drowned insects or emerging bugs.

Wiggle Cast – A cast in which the angler moves the rod tip side to side while shooting line to introduce slack, helping to reduce drag.

Wind Resistance – A factor affecting casting that can be mitigated by using shorter leaders or heavier flies.

Wrist Break – Excessive wrist movement that causes the rod tip to drop too far back, leading to poor loop formation and casting inefficiency.

X

X-System (Tippet Rating) – A numerical system that determines the diameter and strength of the tippet, where smaller numbers indicate thicker, stronger material.

Y

Yarn Strike Indicator – A highly sensitive, adjustable indicator made of wool or synthetic material for detecting subtle strikes.

Z

Zingers: Retractable cords that keep essential tools like nippers and hemostats within easy reach.

Made in the USA
Coppell, TX
30 January 2026

70515433R00085